ANFIELD RISING

**FROM THE LANCASHIRE LEAGUE
TO LEAGUE CHAMPIONS**

ANFIELD
RISING

LIVERPOOL:
THE FIRST DECADE

BRIAN BELTON

Pennant Books

First published in paperback 2008
by Pennant Books

Text copyright © 2008 Brian Belton

British Library Cataloguing-in-Publication Data:
A catalogue record for this book is available on request from
The British Library

ISBN 978-1-906015-25-1

Design & Typeset by Envy Design Ltd

Printed and bound in Great Britian by Creative Print & Design, Blaina, Wales

Pictures reproduced with kind permission of Getty Images and the author.

Every reasonable effort has been made to acknowledge the ownership of
copyright material included in this book. Any errors that have inadvertently
occurred will be corrected in subsequent editions provided notification is
sent to the publisher.

Pennant Books
A division of Pennant Publishing Ltd
PO Box 5675
London W1A 3FB

www.pennantbooks.com

CONTENTS

A FAN'S FOREWORD

BY ANN MORISY

I'm not sure I should have accepted an invitation to write an introduction to a book about the football team I was born to support. Why? Like so many others, I have watched lots and lots of games and have screamed in delight and dismay. But what do I remember most overall?

I recall so many occasions when my life has been given an extraordinary zest – and sometimes grief – because of Liverpool Football Club.

The first occasion was painting the kerbstones red and white in our street and twisting and twirling the crepe paper to decorate the windows in readiness for the street party to celebrate Liverpool winning the FA Cup. This was way back in 1965.

The journey to Wembley in 1965 coincided with my first year at the Grammar School, and even Bootle Grammar School for Girls got caught up in the passion and tension. We girls were cajoled by brothers and fathers to duck out of double French and queue up at Anfield on their behalf as the tickets for the next round went on sale. The thinking went that teachers in the Girls' School were unlikely to know about the frenzy that was about to engulf Anfield and 'a rash that me mother thinks might be German Measles' would give us better cover than our brothers or Dad could provide as they risked 'throwing a sickie'.

Just as people of my generation can recollect where they were and what they were doing when President Kennedy was shot, Liverpool fans also know where they were when the tragedies of the 1980s happened. I was in a caravan park in Brittany at the time of the Heysel Disaster, watching on French telly – and we couldn't make sense of what was going on. When we began to grasp what might be happening, the blame was being heaped upon the 'unruly', 'unreliable' Liverpool fans. That was me and mine they were talking about!

But it got worse. In 1989, it was Hillsborough. For me, it was a sunny afternoon in my little back garden in Derby, with the radio alongside to accompany me as I tackled the weeds. The tears still well up as I think about it. Surely there can be no football club in the world that breaks your heart in the way that Liverpool FC does?

And there was another private sadness in 1986; that was the year my mum died. Now my Mum was an Evertonian – a bold act of rebelliousness in a Protestant family. And as an Evertonian you had to make friends with disappointment, but 1986 was different. In 1986, Everton got to the Final of the FA Cup – only to have to face the might of Liverpool FC. As Saturday drew near, the fellow patients in my mum's ward in Walton Hospital all began to sport their allegiances – Mum in her royal-blue nightdress with a giant rosette, and blue and white plastic boater. When Saturday came, I vowed to shout for Everton – aware that this would be Mum's last season – what a culmination of a lifetime's support it would be for her to have her team lift the FA Cup. My support for Everton lasted for 10 minutes – I'm sorry, Mum, but I know you understand ...

Oh, and then that awesome night in 2005 when Liverpool took on AC Milan in the Final of the Champions League. I had watched them play each round – doing the ironing. But there was no way I was doing the ironing for the Final – it warranted total attention. The waves of dismay flowed repeatedly in that first half. We were 3–0 down at half-time and I wasn't going to waste my time any more and out came the ironing board ... and once again the goals came and Stevie worked his magic! Normal service was resumed because I was in my usual position – behind the ironing board!

So thank you, Liverpool FC, for the innocence of chanting 'Eee ai adido, We Won the Cup' through-out my teenage years.

Thank you, Liverpool FC, for providing me with the unexpected solidarity with the Eritrean guy on the 109 bus who like me has supported the Reds all his life – beginning as a child growing up in Keren.

Thank you, Liverpool FC, for the times I've dashed to get to a telly (anywhere will do) to catch the match and savour the delicious sense of hope that wells up and endures right up to the final whistle – and lasts a lifetime.

INTRODUCTION

Liverpool Football Club will always rank among the great names of the history of the sport. Over the past half-century, the club's achievements and personality have become almost legendary, even among those with little or no interest in football. However, it seems the origins of the club and how they made their way during the first days of their existence are steeped in ambiguity.

This book charts the very first years of one of the great success stories of the beautiful game. From creation to promotion and on to the Liverpool Reds' first League Championship, this is the story of a time when the first seeds of success were planted on what was to be the fertile turf of Stanley Park and what would become the Anfield legend.

The story is a fascinating saga of the making of a colossus of the realm of sport, showing how the foundations were laid for the great powerhouse of football that Liverpool were to become. At the same time, it is a challenge to the notion that Liverpool Football Club grew out of Everton FC, a version of events that has been repeatedly penned by committed and knowledgeable historians of the noble Toffees. The most neutral description of how one club became two was that the parting of the ways came about a bit like cell division; one made two. But a deeper analysis of what occurred leaves one with the impression that Liverpool, in fact, gave rise to Everton and that, like Chelsea around 13 years later, Liverpool arose out of their ground, the place that Everton left behind. Anfield was forsaken and most of the crown jewels of the team that first played there and even the very name of the club (despite some resistance) were taken like booty to Goodison Park. Indeed, it is only a matter of circumstance that what was in effect the deserting party held on to the Everton name, which just as easily could have stayed at Anfield. Although many 'institutional facets' remained in place – principally the ground, but also much of the bureaucratic structure, the club president John Houlding, its first secretary (effectively the club manager) William Barclay and one of the great architects of the first glory days of Liverpool FC John McKenna – Everton effectively 'abandoned ship', leaving those who remained to their fate. In fact, those who effected the Everton exodus did all they could to stifle their neighbours from the very start.

This was made evident when the 16 April 1892 edition of the *Liverpool Echo* reported, 'Mr Houlding had applied for an interim injunction against George Mahon, Dr Baxter, John Atkinson and William R Clayton [men central to orchestrating Everton's recent departure from Anfield] to prevent them from removing any of the fixtures and fittings already in place at Anfield.'

George Mahon was one of those that led the walk-out along with Dr James Clement Baxter, and perhaps the intentions of Mahon and his lads were understandable, given the Anfield club's close proximity to and shared constituency with the relocated Everton. It is possible that feelings of 'ownership' of what they had helped to build had motivated these men to attempt to rip the guts out of Anfield.

Mahon had joined the club in 1889 and was to take a big role in the first part of Everton's League history. Baxter was well respected among Liverpool's Irish Catholic community and his influence in establishing Everton's connections with Catholicism were considerable. Educated at St Francis Xavier College, he became a physician of some repute, and, from 1906 to 1920, he represented the Liberal Party on the City Council. During his time with Everton, Baxter was to take a number of positions, including medical adviser, director and chairman.

Baxter and Mahon, like their allies, ostensibly 'set up shop' elsewhere because they didn't want to stand by and watch Houlding make what they saw as excessive profit out of the club. It was also rumoured that Mahon and others, who had been involved with the club from their beginnings as a church team, found the association with Houlding, a publican and brewer, unseemly. But there was more to the breakaway than this and, if one is to understand Liverpool, the background and what led up to the 'great schism' needs to be analysed.

The Goodison Park club, although sharing a common footballing history with Liverpool, were, if anything, at root, a creation of Houlding; Everton blossomed out of the dirt of Anfield Park, a venue forever to be associated with the Liverpool Reds. To this extent, Everton can be understood to be the progeny of Liverpool Football Club.

The 1892 *Liverpool Echo* report provides a good idea of what Anfield looked like at the time one club became two: 'the ground contains four large stands for spectators, one on each of the said piece of land. The stand on the north side measures about 50 yards in length, the stand on the east side measures 65 yards in length, the stand on the south side (Kemlyn Road) measures about 125 yards in length and the stand on the west side about 60 yards in length. All the said stands are built practically on the same lines – viz, columns of brickwork were built into the ground, such columns rising from the height of a few bricks at the point nearest to the centre of the ground in steps till they reach the outside edge of the land at which point they are of a considerable height. On each of the steps there are beams of timber extending under the next step and firmly built into the brickwork with mortar. The cross-planking in which the people stand and sit is nailed down and securely fastened to the said beams of timber and further secured to uprights which are let into the ground. Eight wooden buildings or sheds containing iron turnstiles surrounded by a hoarding are fixed into the soil to a considerable depth.'

This was the citadel within which Liverpool were conceived and wrought.

The club's story doesn't start with the so-called 'split' and Everton leaving Anfield. To know the authentic tale of the development of Liverpool FC, one has to know how the club came to be based at Anfield. For some years, Liverpool and Everton were one. As Manchester United were the progeny of Newton Heath, West Ham United grew out of Thames Ironworks and Arsenal were preceded by Woolwich Arsenal, so Liverpool had a 'forerunner', although, unlike those clubs mentioned, Liverpool's predecessor survived and thrived.

Given the situation, Liverpool can claim a part of anything Everton were before their removal to

Goodison Park; those years, wherein football history was made and glory won, represent a legacy that those for whom Liverpool FC have been part of their way of life need to reclaim as, in part, theirs. To do anything else is to throw away a heritage and deny an ancestral bond; those who *are* Liverpool FC, their supporters, are richer for the knowledge of their actual and accurate history.

As such, what follows is a chronicle that every true Red should know, as the glories of the last half-century and the certain achievements of the future have been and will be built on Liverpool's first days, the time of *Anfield Rising*.

1
GRASS ROOTS IN THE PEOPLE'S PARK

When the Mayor of Liverpool opened Stanley Park in May 1870, he told the 30,000 people who had gathered for the ceremony, 'Although the corporation of Liverpool has several parks, such as the Sheil Park, the Wavertree Park and the Newsham Park, there is no park that has yet been opened to the public which deserves the name of the People's Park more than Stanley Park. When I consider what large masses of people live within the space which stretches from the outskirts of this park down to the Mersey, and the confined habitations in which they dwell, and when I look at the grand scene around me today I cannot but believe that the park will be the greatest benefit in various ways to all classes of the community – a benefit both morally and physically.'

Close to 60 of Stanley Park's 100 acres were given over to sport and leisure and the new park certainly was a welcome open space in a metropolis with one of the lowest ratios of open public space for leisure in Britain, the city having expanded incredibly quickly during the 19th century. A couple of years before the park opened, a government report told how the parliamentary boundary of Liverpool, 7.8 square miles, had a population of 500,860, meaning each acre had around 100 inhabitants, more than twice as many per acre as Manchester and Salford.

At that time, the better-off acquired land for sports; facilities such as swimming baths, cricket fields and Aintree Racecourse were put in place, and the Liverpool Athletic Club organised the Liverpool Olympics in 1862, 1863, 1864 and 1867. For poorer people, long working hours left little time or energy for sport, but, from the 1850s, workers all over Britain began a campaign for the Saturday half-day, although this battle would not be totally won in Liverpool until well into the 1890s.

ANFIELD RISING

Prior to 1860, by far the most popular team sport in Liverpool was cricket, with private cricket clubs, such as Liverpool and Bootle, and, as the sport grew in popularity, the necessity for expansive open public space became ever more pressing. This was met partly by the opening of Wavertree Park in 1856 and Newsham and Sheil Parks towards the end of the 1860s. However, at that time, these areas were not situated in working-class districts, the places where need for open space was greatest.

Sports were pursued all over the district on a range of fields, and over 40 cricket teams existed, which challenges the perception of 19th-century cricket as a mostly middle-class game, and, as workers began to gain the half-day Saturday, more cricket teams were formed in working-class areas. This process was energised by the opening of Stanley Park.

All over Britain, particularly in the Midlands and the North, the new sport of Association Football was gaining ground, and, by the late 1860s/early 1870s, football was progressively becoming a predominantly working-class game. The Birmingham area led the way, which can largely be attributed to the region's achieving the half-day Saturday long before Liverpool, but, by 1878, the first football clubs were being organised in Liverpool.

2
THE BEGINNING

The chronicles of Liverpool Football Club start with their nearest neighbours and, historically, the Reds' biggest rivals.

The shared origin of both Liverpool and Everton can be traced to the English Methodist congregation called New Connexion, a secessionist group from the Wesleyan Methodists, led by Alexander Kilham, that had started in Sheffield, founded in 1797 (some Wesleyans accused Kilham of revolutionary sympathies and links with the renowned republican Tom Paine). In the mid- to late 1860s, Welshman Guto Sion Jones developed a chapel of the congregation in the Liverpool area. In 1869, the church purchased land on Breckfield Road North, between St Domingo Vale and St Domingo Grove (named after St Dominic, another 'questioning cleric', who inspired the Dominican movement). This was located near the district of Everton, which had become part of the city of Liverpool in 1835.

In 1871, three old, decrepit Methodist churches were replaced by the new chapel of St Domingo in Breckfield Road North. The new building included a Sunday school (which had been running since 1870 – the site had been consecrated in May of that year).

The church became the kernel of the local community of working people whose homes nestled around the area. In the first years of the congregation, younger, more progressive curates promoted a spiritual interpretation of the 'healthy mind, healthy body' doctrine as had been advocated by the YMCA (the 'triangle' of mind, body, spirit) for over a quarter of a century.

This 'muscular Christianity', as it would become known, was seen as a means to resist the 'evils' and difficulties that beset working-class urban existence of the time; sport became an essential component of spiritual life right across the spectrum of Christianity in Britain. St Domingo's Sunday school flourished and young people were eager to take part in the range of sporting competitions arranged within and sometimes between dioceses. This was replicated in working-class communities throughout Liverpool and Britain.

St Domingo's boasted a cricket team that played regular matches against other Sunday schools in Liverpool and, six years after St Domingo's was established, a group of young men from the cricket team, looking for something to occupy them during the winter, approached the man who had organised their side, the Reverend Benjamin Swift Chambers, requesting the organisation of a football club. Chambers had not been in the post long but, with the help of George Mahon, an accountant and the church organist, was pleased to work with the lads on their idea. Mahon was born in Liverpool in 1854, but his family relocated to Ireland when he was a child, where he was educated. He returned to Liverpool where he later became a senior partner in Roose, Mahon & Howard, a leading firm of accountants, in fact one of Liverpool's most successful.

In the last quarter of the 19th century, rugby was the most popular of the winter sports in Liverpool, but there was a growing interest in football, and in 1878 the St Domingo's Football Club was founded. The team played their first match in the southeast corner of Stanley Park; the players carried homemade goalposts from the Park Lodge on Mill Lane and slotted them into metal sockets placed at either end of a patch of rough ground. They then marked out the field of play, a much less complex job than it is today, and not far off jumpers for goalposts.

St Domingo's played all their home games in Stanley Park. Their first fixtures were organised in a largely informal way, but the side quickly found their feet and a spirit of healthy competition was promoted between local teams. Anyone could wander up to the side of the pitch to watch matches – no one in Liverpool (or most other places) had thought of charging people to view the games at this point. Saint Ds (as they came to be known) swiftly generated a local reputation and increasingly gifted players were recruited from beyond the parish with little or no affiliation to the church.

In just 12 months, bolstered by their achievements, the St Domingo's Football Club, determined to widen their area of influence, thought about adopting a more encompassing title for their club. In November 1879, the meeting at which it was decided to assume a new name for St Domingo's took place at the Queens Head Hotel in Village Street, off Everton Road, not far from the old bridewell lock-up tower (known as Prince Rupert's tower) that is still depicted on the Everton club crest today. The Everton Football Club epithet was picked and the team played their debut match under this name at Stanley Park on 20 December vs. St Peter's; the 6–0 result was Everton's first win. The team was: W Jones; T Evans, J Douglas, C Hiles, S Chalk (captain), RW Morris, A White, F Brettle, A Wade, Smith, W Williams.

It was not usual at this time for teams to wear uniform colours. Players on the same side could wear any colours they had (or wished) which predictably led to a deal of confusion. Later, Everton, seeing the advantages of players being able to quickly identify each other as well as members of opposing teams, looked to create a set of matching shirts while avoiding buying a complete set of new ones. This involved dyeing black all the various shirts that their players wore. A two-inch-wide scarlet sash worn around the waist finished off the look, and the side became known as 'The Black Watch', in recognition of the famous regiment, but also probably because some of the previous colours of the shirts started to reappear after being drenched during play and washed a few times, so at a distance looked a bit like Black Watch tartan. Other colours were used over the years and the club didn't settle for royal blue until the 1901/02 campaign.

The club's secretary, JW Clarke, organised games against sides from all over the Liverpool district and the team continued to do well. This being the case, the side attracted some of the best players in the city. Although the club no longer bore the name of the church, it maintained connections with St Domingo's. In fact, as late as 1928, a service was held at the church to mark the club's jubilee.

On the strength of consistently good performances, Everton had become part of the Lancashire Association by 1880 and were competing against sides as distant as Bolton and

Birkenhead. Home matches continued to be contested on the public pitch in Stanley Park.

Now, as a member of the County FA, the club were able to supplement their friendly contests by taking part in the Lancashire Cup (their first serious contest), and in the first round of their initial outing in this competition they drew Great Lever, a well-established side from the Bolton area. A laudable 1–1 away draw was followed by an 8–1 mauling, but, on finding out that the referee (who had made a string of odd decisions during the drubbing, none in the home team's favour) was a member of the Great Lever committee, Everton lodged a protest which was upheld by the Lancashire FA. It was a discontented Great Lever crowd that 'welcomed' Everton for the third match of the tie. The visitors eventually lost by the only goal of the game and made their way home with the expletives that had been directed at them by the home supporters throughout the match ringing in their ears.

3
ENTER HOULDING

The opening result of the 1881/82 season could hardly have been worse for the new club. Bolton Wanderers, just four years older, smashed the Mersey men 13-1. The result prompted the organisation of a new training regime, watched over by the side's centre-forward and skipper Jack McGill, formerly of Glasgow Rangers. Added fitness and skill sessions were undertaken in the evening. As their efforts mostly took place on the dark winter nights, the side soon became known as the 'Moonlight Dribblers'.

The Liverpool district boasted a fine bunch of entrants for that season's Lancashire Cup: Bootle, Liverpool Association and St Peter's joined

Everton, who started the competition well with a 5-0 win over Middleton at Stanley Park to go on to face Turton in the next round. Situated close to Blackburn, Turton were established in 1871 and as such were the oldest club in Lancashire and still exist today. On this occasion, they proved to be too strong for Everton.

At this time, Bootle were Everton's biggest rivals, but Everton won the first two meetings between the sides, 7-4 at Stanley Park and 4-1 on Bootle's turf.

With 15 wins from 22 matches, plus four draws, Everton had a good season. They scored 70 goals while letting in just 16 and had become known as a good side, at times attracting in excess of 2,000 people in Stanley Park. The need for an enclosed ground was becoming evident, allowing for entrance fees to be taken, but the club's hand was forced during 1882 when a new Lancashire Association regulation obliged their member clubs to play their games on enclosed grounds.

In March 1882, a meeting took place at the Sandon Hotel in Everton (where all the club meetings were held). Built in 1881, the Sandon is situated on the corner of Oakfield Road and Houlding Street, named after the first owner of the hotel John Houlding. A self-made man, Houlding started working life in a brewery, but, after he bought the Sandon, the business did well enough to generate the finance for him to purchase a small brewery of his own. Houlding, whose impressive political biography included time as an alderman, a Justice of the Peace and Mayor of Liverpool, was enthusiastic about football and would have a big influence on the development of both Liverpool and Everton over the coming few years. He allowed Everton to use the Sandon for social events and meetings; it doubled as the team's changing rooms and most of the early photographs of the side were taken on the hotel's bowling green. A plaque inside the hotel records its place in the history of both Everton and Liverpool Football Clubs.

At that March meeting, it was decided that a field off Priory Road, next to the pitch the club used in Stanley Park, should be rented. It was offered to the club by wealthy cattle importer and club member William Cruitt whose house adjoined the area.

The 1882/83 term, Everton's fourth campaign, saw football become better organised in the Liverpool area as the thirst for more competitive games grew; the Lancashire Cup was just not enough and so a dozen sides from the area formed the Liverpool and District Football Association and launched the Liverpool Senior Cup in the 1882/83 term.

Everton suffered a swift exit from the Lancashire Cup, at the hands of Blackburn Rovers, one of the best sides in England during that period, so the 8–0 result was not as bad as it looks, particularly viewed alongside the Rovers' recent 16–0 destruction of Preston North End. Just the previous season, Rovers had made themselves the first Northern side to compete in an FA Cup Final (although they were defeated by the Old Etonians, it was by the only goal of the game).

The first Liverpool Senior Cup saw Everton eliminated 3–1 by Bootle, and the Bucks went on to win the trophy. Proceeds from this competition were donated to the Hospital Saturday Fund and all the matches had good crowds.

The last game of the season was the end of Everton's time in Stanley Park, the true birthplace of football in Liverpool, although this was not the end of the game there. Many other teams were now using the park, with a growing spectator interest.

4

THE FIRST TROPHY

The first official match at Priory Road was played in October 1883 between a Liverpool and District team (consisting of Everton players) and Walsall and District side; the match ended in a 3-3 draw. However, the attendance at that initial game was poor (raising just 14 shillings in gate receipts). The first club side to visit the Priory Road ground was Hartford St Johns (a Northwich side). Everton beat them 3-1, Jack McGill scoring the first Everton goal at the club's new home.

The playing area at Priory Road was 200 yards long and 100 yards wide (the modern incarnation of football pitches that includes a penalty area, centre circle and so on did not exist - the first standardisation of pitches wasn't enacted until 1892). There were railings protecting the pitch and a shed was built as a rough and ready changing room. A makeshift stand was constructed for club officials with a few seats for better-off spectators; entrance fees were collected outside the ground.

A fortnight after the defeat of St Johns, the strong North Midlands side Burslem Port Vale came to Liverpool. The 50 miles Burslem travelled was the furthest any team had trekked to meet an Everton XI, and it was worthwhile as they beat the home side 1–0 in a tight match. A return game was played in December and, despite making the longest trip the club have ever made, they achieved a fine 2–2 draw in a very entertaining match.

Between the encounters with Burslem Port Vale, Everton had made an excellent start to their Liverpool Senior Cup campaign with a 10–0 win against old rivals St Peter's. And a 4–1 victory over Liverpool Ramblers led to a third-round away tie against Bootle Wanderers. However, Bootle opted to stage the match at Priory Road. This was seemingly a mistake, as Everton won 5–2. At this stage just three teams were left in the competition. Earlestown were drawn to meet Liverpool Stanley while Everton were given a bye. Stanley were beaten 2–1 so it was Earlestown and Everton who fought it out for the trophy.

The Final was played on 29 March 1884 at Bootle's new Hawthorne Road ground (at that point the football club were sharing the facility with Bootle Cricket Club). A good crowd of 2,500 turned up for the Final that kicked off at 3.30 p.m.

The first half finished goalless. There were 25 minutes left to play when Everton's Edwin Berry tore down the left flank. Berry's cross was met by a confused defence which allowed WH Parry to zip in and claim the winning goal. The Liverpool Senior Cup was the club's first trophy.

Everton's stay at Priory Road was to be a temporary sojourn, as it seemed the once benevolent Cruitt was not keen on the close company of raucous supporters.

John Houlding, who had recently been appointed club president, found the side a new pitch alongside Walton Breck Road, the former home of Everton Cricket Club; it was part of an area in Anfield owned by brothers John and Joseph Orrell, Houlding's fellow brewers. The brothers owned two fields there and the one belonging to Joseph (not John as many contemporary accounts have insisted; see Keats, 1929, p15, Roberts, 1978, p24) became Everton's third home, with Houlding as the 'representative tenant'. This in effect meant that he was renting the land for the club's use.

The terms for the occupation of the ground stipulated that the football club would keep the existing walls in good repair, pay the taxes and not be 'a nuisance' to Orrell and other neigh-bouring tenants. It was also agreed that the club would pay a modest rent, or 'subscribe a donation each year to the Stanley Hospital in the name of Mr Orrell'.

Before the start of the new season, club members and players set to work to prepare the ground. The open field was transformed into an enclosed football pitch by the construction of a fence around it. A modest stand was erected on the east side for officials, club members and the press, while a few seats were put in for better-off supporters at the ground that would be known as Anfield.

5

TO ANFIELD

Everton's debut game at Anfield was against Earlestown at 3.40 p.m. on 27 September 1884, with the home side winning 5-0 in front of a good crowd. The team Everton fielded that day was: Lindsay; Marriott, Morris, Pickering, Preston, Richards, Parry, Gibson, Whittle, McGill and Higgins.

Mike Higgins became the first player to score at Anfield, with Everton's other goals claimed by Whittle (2), Gibson and Richards.

However, Everton's season had begun with an invitation game against Burslem Port Vale to celebrate the opening of their new ground, where an understrength side were beaten 7-0.

The Liverpool and District Association now boasted 36 teams and as such the Liverpool Senior Cup presented a much more challenging competition. Everton began their defence of the trophy with a 7–0 win over Toxteth Wanderers (who were based at Sefton Park). They then got past Southport, Bootle and Golbourne to put themselves in the Final for the second successive season.

The Final was again staged at Bootle's Hawthorne Road ground and once more Everton faced Earlestown who won the game 1–0, although Everton had much more of the play. Indeed, practically everyone in the ground had thought the holders had scored an equaliser, but an umpire had not agreed.

In the 1880s, two umpires (generally one nominated from each of the sides contesting a game) worked with the referee to control the match. It was not until 1891 that the Football Association ruled that the referee would be the first and final arbiter of the rules during matches. It was also at this point that it became no longer necessary for players to appeal to the referee for a decision; from then on the official could award free-kicks at his own discretion (before this time players had to query incidents with officials before they would utter a word). Each of the competing clubs was still able to nominate an umpire to help the referee but they were limited to working from the touchlines. These 'assistant referees' were eventually referred to as 'linesman'. Neutral linesmen for important matches were only introduced in the 1898/99 season.

So, the first Anfield season concluded with disappointment but the club had secured a permanent home and a healthy income; £200 was taken at the gate, an £155 improvement on the 1883/84 term.

Up to the mid-1880s, football was still officially an amateur game, but most successful clubs were beginning to employ professional players. Everton had avoided taking on the full mantle of professionalism but for some time it had been clear that this would be the way of things in the future, even if some diehards in the South of England would continue the fight until after World War I to keep the game 'free from the stain of filthy lucre'. A number of teams refused to accept the professional game and the likes of Darwen, Great Lever, Earlestown and Bootle (the Bootle side of today have no direct links with the latter) vanished into the mists of history. However, others, such as Liverpool Ramblers, continued to operate, albeit at the lower levels of football.

Everton became fully professional during 1885 along with many other leading English clubs when the FA lifted the ban on professionalism. Competition for success and the need to attract and keep the best players demanded higher income. Everton's first batch of openly professional players were George Dobson, a full-back who had come to the club from Bolton Wanderers, George Farmer from Oswestry and Alec Dick who joined the club from Kilmarnock.

Everton prospered with Houlding providing generous financial support and crowds of over 8,000 attending games to watch consistently good results. Houlding's initial involvement would probably have been about attracting the players and their supporters to his hostelry and perhaps gaining a little promotion for his business from being associated with the team, although he undoubtedly also had a passion for the game. As the club began to look like a profitable concern in their own right, Houlding's lively business instinct would have begun to understand the financial potential of football in general and Everton in particular. This goes some way to explaining his growing investment in the club and their ground. By 1886, the increase in crowd size motivated Houlding to build a new stand at a cost of around £64. He employed George Rutherford, a local builder, to construct the stand on the Kemlyn Road side of the ground (which would become the site of the Centenary Stand). Also prior to Everton's 1886/87 campaign, the perimeter fence that surrounded Anfield was heightened. This latter work, which was finished by 6 August 1886, cost the grand total of £34 2s 6d. A covered stand was erected on the opposite side of the ground. More groundwork continued in the last part of the 1880s including the building of two stands (one behind each goal). The ground was by that time one of the finest in the country, a fact that was recognised when the stadium hosted its first international game in 1889.

There was a poor start to the 1885/86 campaign, when East Lancashire sides Bolton Wanderers and Rawtenstall came to Anfield and won. The Lancashire FA demoted Everton to the Junior Cup, a newly initiated competition.

The Junior Cup (also know as the Lancashire Football Association Challenge Trophy) does not, as the modern understanding might suggest, refer to a youth tournament. (The first football organised specifically for youngsters would have been called 'schoolboy'.) The Junior Cup was a sort of second-division equivalent for Lancashire clubs and it is likely that the decision to place Everton in this tournament rather than the new 'Senior' incarnation was that bigger/richer/better politically placed clubs would have taken up the upper echelon. Having two cups also provided more income while giving two Lancashire clubs (rather than one) a chance of glory.

In the first round of the Junior Cup, Adlington came to Anfield to be destroyed 8–1. Under-estimating their opponents in the next round, Everton went to Peel Park with something of a second team and lost 5–1.

The next weekend, Everton made their first visit to North Wales to meet the Druids who had eliminated Bolton Wanderers from the FA Cup in 1883. The Welshmen won 4–0. On New Year's Day 1886, Anfield welcomed its first Scottish visitors, Partick Thistle, who left 3–0 victors. The next day

Everton played host to their first 'overseas' opponents, Irish side Limavady, who beat them 1–0.

Everton made the short trip to meet Bootle at Hawthorne Road on 23 January. The home side conceded a goal early on and, with George Dobson playing a blinder in the Everton defence, Bootle were allowed no reply.

In February, Everton progressed well in the Liverpool Senior Cup, overcoming Southport Wanderers and then New Ferry. This led to a tie with High Park, a Southport-based side. Everton arrived to find 800 locals willing their side on, although, with the first half played, the visitors were leading 2–0. But by the end Everton were thankful to have held on to win the match 2–1, owing a great deal to the performance of George Dobson.

Everton's semi-final opponents at Hawthorne Road were Liverpool Stanley. A fine crowd of around 5,000, producing an £80 gate, saw Everton win 3–0 and pave the way to meet Bootle in the Final at Walton Stiles (Liverpool Stanley's ground). It wasn't the biggest of grounds but they crammed in 8,000 for the game.

Bootle kicked off and the match started as a

pretty even contest; it took a fine shot from Everton's Gibson to separate the sides at half-time. At the start of the second half, as Bootle threw themselves forward in waves at the Everton goal, the side's skipper, Eyton Jones, was in torturing form on the left wing. But yet again George Dobson was a giant in defence and he was not ready to concede the Final for a second year; Everton managed to hold on to win Anfield's first trophy.

To celebrate the opening of their Prescot Road ground, Liverpool Athletic Club organised a competition over the late May Bank Holiday to be staged at their new home. Eight clubs were invited to compete but it was the form sides, Everton and Bootle, that met in the Final. A crowd of around 8,000 people attended the late Monday evening match.

Bootle seemed resolved to seek retribution for their failure in the Liverpool Senior Cup, and they grabbed the lead early on and held it up to the end of the first half. Early in the second half, the match was levelled. A shot from George Farmer met the fist of Galbraith, but the Anfielders claimed the Bootle keeper had connected with the ball after it had crossed the line. Mr WH Bailey, the referee, agreed and confirmed the equaliser. The Bootle players and officials were up in arms, but to no avail. When the game recommenced, the Bucks players made a string of attacks on their opponents' goal. Twice Bootle had appeals for goals turned down and as the game wore on their poise ran dangerously low and drained completely away when Wilding put Everton 2–1 up.

Nevertheless, at full-time, Bootle totally denied that they had been defeated and Liverpool Athletic decided to hold on to the winner's shield, choosing to leave it to the Liverpool and District Committee to sort out. Ultimately, Everton were awarded the shield.

6

FROM BOOTLE
TO BELFAST

The Anfield club started the new season with nine successive home games (there was either no reason for this or the logic has been lost over time). Again Everton took part in the Lancashire Junior Cup competition, meeting Fleetwood Zingari ('Zingari' means 'Gypsy' in Italian), and the Romany-inspired estuary men were beaten 9–0.

Next up was a visit from Bells Temperance. A crowd of 1,500 welcomed the Accrington-based visitors to Anfield. Everton fielded just three regular first-teamers for the match and consequently the teetotallers won 3–2 (which was probably not quite enough to drive the Everton men to drink).

In the Liverpool Senior Cup, Everton met Bootle

and it seemed something of a shame that one of the two best sides in the district would be eliminated so soon. About 10,000 turned up for the game. Bootle kicked off and were the better team over the first 45 minutes but the half finished goalless. The match was interrupted a number of times as supporters spilled on to the field of play as a direct result of overcrowding.

After the break, the home side continued to turn the screw and before long it seemed like Bootle had broken the deadlock but on umpire intervention the ball was deemed to have gone wide. There were 25 minutes of the game left when the visitors went one up. The Bootle keeper was unable to hold on to a cross from the left wing and Briscoe took advantage.

Looking desperate, Bootle committed to seek to level the game. George Dobson made a goal-line clearance to preserve his side's lead before play was held up, while, yet again, stewards cleared the pitch of supporters. When the match resumed, it looked as if Bootle's concentration had been affected as Everton scored a second after a goalmouth skirmish. With 90 seconds left on the clock, the crowd surged on to the pitch for the final time. When the playing area was finally cleared, the

Bootle side had got changed and refused to play out the game, so Everton were declared winners.

When Tranmere Rovers were beaten 9–1, Everton went to the Final of the Liverpool Senior Cup for the fourth successive year. The game would once more be staged at Hawthorne Road; this time Everton would face Oakfield Rovers, a side mostly made up of players that had previously played for Anfield Road Sunday school.

However, with Bootle out of the running, fewer than 3,000 watched the Final that ended in an easy 5–0 victory for Everton; the Liverpool Senior Cup returned to Anfield with Everton winning the trophy for the third time in the half-decade the competition had been running.

Anfield featured in the FA Cup for the first time that season; however, at that time, professional players were required to be registered with a club for a particular period and several of the Everton first-team members did not meet this condition. The side were drawn to meet the powerful Glasgow Rangers (this was a time when Scottish clubs took part in the FA Cup) at Anfield. But Everton decided to withdraw from the competition rather than breach the rules or field a weakened team.

In the end, the game with the Gers was played as a friendly and around 6,000 people turned up for the encounter, the biggest crowd Anfield had seen. The Glasgow Blues won 1–0 (scoring in the first quarter-of-an-hour) but after the break Everton had struck a post and all in all had held their own against one of the powerhouses of British football.

Over the Christmas period, Everton met the legendary amateur side Corinthians, the first London club to visit Liverpool, who were a quality side – in fact, on a number of occasions the England national side had been entirely made up of Corinthians players. It was snowing when they arrived in Liverpool but a crowd of over 3,000 braved the Anfield weather in order to view some of the finest players in the country. Everton did well to score twice and only let in four.

During Easter, Everton journeyed overseas for the first time, making the trip to Northern Ireland to meet an 'Ulster Select' XI in Belfast. The match was due to be staged on the Saturday, but Everton's ship was held up due to fog on the Mersey. As such the game was played on Easter Monday at the Ballynafiegh Cricket Ground, where a big crowd saw Everton win 2–1 with goals from Gibson and Dobson.

7

LEAGUE FOOTBALL

O n 15 October 1887, Everton made their first 'real' foray into the FA Cup. The first round took them to meet Bolton (500 Anfielders followed their team across the county for the match – a big pilgrimage for the time). The game was played at a furious pace, both sides seemingly committed to an attacking game, but there was no score at half-time. The second half brought much the same, but, when a high ball into the Everton area from the left was cleverly slotted home by Roberts, the visitors had to double their efforts. However, Bolton held firm to win the game.

The indignant Everton secretary, Alexander Nesbit, made an appeal to the FA, arguing that a

Bolton player had been late registering. Subsequently, the match was replayed to a draw and a second replay concluded in the same way. On 19 November, Bolton were beaten 2–1 at Anfield.

A trip to meet Preston North End was the enticing prospect offered by the next round, but this was postponed as the Wanderers claimed that Everton had 'persuaded players to join them by financial inducement' (having paid seven of their registered 'amateurs'). The tie at Deepdale was played while the FA worked on the issue. In the previous round, North End had defeated Hyde United 26–0 to record the highest score in any official match (FA Cup or Football League) ever played in England, which still stands.

Everton made a number of changes to the side that won in the preceding round. The visitors kicked off but the home team were in front by the fourth minute, and Preston had doubled their lead by half-time. After the interval, the Merseysiders hardly got out of their own half and ended up losing the game 6–0.

More bad news came when the FA declared that seven of Everton's 'amateur' players were in reality professional (while professionalism was no longer outlawed at this time, many strictures were placed on fielding professionals, for example, different rules for registration). Everton were suspended for a month by the FA and the Liverpool Association sent Bob Lythgoe, a former goalkeeper and football administrator locally, to the Sandon Hotel to retrieve the Liverpool Senior Cup (won by the Anfield side the previous season) from the hotel entrance where it had been placed in celebration of Everton's achievement. A local mason was to place a gravestone where the trophy had been proudly displayed. It read: 'SACRED TO THE MEMORY OF THE LIVERPOOL CUP WHICH WAS WON BY THE EVERTON CLUB, 1884, 1886 AND 1887 AND TAKEN FROM THEM BY THE LIVERPOOL DISTRICT ASSOCIATION, APRIL 1888. "GONE BUT NOT FORGOTTEN."'

By way of protest, Everton temporarily resigned from the Liverpool and District Football Association and refused to enter their competition the following season.

However, in February 1888, the FA staged one of the Cup semi-finals at Anfield, the first time the city of Liverpool had been given such an honour. The match between Crewe Alexandra and Preston North End attracted a crowd of about 10,000;

Preston won 5-0 but lost in the Final to West Bromwich Albion.

The saga of the Cup showed up the limitations that many of the leading clubs in the North and Midlands felt were holding them back in terms of their commercial development and ability to compete, and in 1888 they formed the Football League. Six teams from the North West and the same number from the Midlands were invited to take part in the initial season. Although the Lancashire Association questioned Everton's overall ability, the Anfield side took their place alongside Accrington, Aston Villa, Blackburn Rovers, Bolton Wanderers, Burnley, Derby County, Notts County, Preston North End, Stoke, West Bromwich Albion and Wolverhampton Wanderers as the founder members of the Football League. Two points would be awarded for a win and one for a draw.

Behind the scenes, the Everton executive asked for a lease on Anfield on 24 July 1888, so that investment in stands and accommodation would benefit the club and they suspended work on the construction of new stands until the matter was settled.

In the first years of Everton's stay at Anfield,

John Houlding was the 'representative tenant', having leased the land from Orrell in his own name, but when the club became part of the Football League, with the accompanying increase in crowds and so revenue, the club became a much more attractive proposition as a potential profit-making business. From the start of Everton's time at Anfield, Houlding had effectively taken on the role of 'landlord' by deciding to sub-let Anfield to Everton. Using his representative-tenant status, he ended the nominal tenancy with the warning that if the club's income increased so would the rent. There was nothing stopping him charging the club whatever he wanted for their use of the land.

Although Houlding was president of the club, he refused Everton's request for a lease; however, he told the executive that, as long as they paid what he saw as a fair rent and did not meddle with the boundary walls (unless he gave permission), Everton's future tenancy of Anfield would be secure. He also demanded a monopoly over the refreshments sold at Anfield, stipulating in the tenancy agreement that the landlord (Houlding) should have the sole right of supply.

At the same time, Houlding attempted to

persuade the committee to agree to purchase land belonging to both Orrell brothers and a further 15,000 square yards that Houlding himself had bought and offered for £6,000 – £3,000 of which he wanted to be left on mortgage, at 4 per cent.

There are no records detailing Houlding's intentions but it seems clear that he was looking to consolidate his position at the club. But discontent was growing among the executive.

Everton made their League debut on 8 September 1888 in front of 10,000 supporters at Anfield, vs. Accrington (no direct relation to Stanley, who were not founded for another three years). The Everton line-up was: RH Smalley; N Ross, A Dick, G Dobson, J Holt, B Jones, G Farmer, E Chadwick, W Lewis, D Waugh and G Fleming.

No goals were scored in the first half and the sides looked pretty evenly matched. But in the second half Everton took the lead – the club's first League goal came from a header by George Fleming. The same player got Everton's second and the home side came out 2–1 winners.

At the start of November, Everton were in third place in the League but, with just three wins from their last 13 games, they finished their inaugural League season in eighth place, narrowly avoiding the need to apply for re-election by three points.

Inconsistency, partly attributable to constant alterations to the side (35 players were deployed in the 22 matches), and a lack of goals (Everton hit just 35 in that first campaign while conceding 46) had been the club's main problems. Away from Anfield, they had scored only 11 times and lost eight of their 11 games.

Qualifying rounds were introduced in the FA Cup in the 1888/89 season. Everton's draw presented a trip to Ulster. But the cost of travelling across the sea caused them to withdraw from the competition.

In August 1888, William E Barclay became Everton's first club secretary (as close as the early game came to a manager and, up to 1939, Everton's club secretary would be responsible for selecting the team) and he swiftly brought good players such as John Holt, Alf Milward, Edgar Chadwick and Nick Ross to the club. Ross was one of the best defenders of his day and it was rumoured that he was handsomely paid, in the order of £10 a month (this was a time when a miner, working perhaps 60 hours a week, might expect to earn £1). Other team members received around half this sum (if they were lucky). The left-wing partnership of Milward and Chadwick would be recognised as one of the most effective in the League. Holt came to Anfield from Bootle, a side unfortunate not to have been invited to join the League. Johnny was a central defender, powerful in the air and a superb man-to-man marker, and he would play around 225 League games for Everton.

Anfield staged its first international game on 3 March 1889, when England met Ireland. England won the game 6–1 watched by a rather unsatisfactory 6,000 people, although the poor attendance might have been due to Everton's John Holt failing to be selected for the England side.

The continuing power struggle at the club was beginning to become more obvious. Complaints about Houlding's sway over the club erupted into open anguish when members decided to form the club into a limited liability company with the aim of purchasing the Everton Football Ground (Anfield). This was put in the form of an official resolution at a special committee meeting held on 22 May 1889 and defeated by Houlding and his supporters. Again, we can only speculate on Houlding's motivations given the limited information that exists about events at Anfield close to 120 years ago, but it appears that this arrangement could never suit Houlding, as it was much more limited than his previous proposal and did not include the entire area in which he had a personal financial interest. It also seems reasonable to conclude that the timing was not right for Houlding who feared that the formation of a limited liability company at this time could have prevented him from making any claims on the club's assets (which, from his perspective, given his history of substantial investments in the club, might well have seemed unfair) and would have ended his 'right' to demand rent at a level that he saw as appropriate to the club's status/income and recompense for his past investment. However, the debate was to prove to be just the opening shots in a long battle for control of the club. Houlding and his allies had the advantage; when they 'won the day', they were able to continue dictating the sub-let rent, at least for the time being.

8
LIVERPOOL'S GLORY

Richard Molyneux took charge of team matters at Anfield in September 1889, replacing Barclay who remained a member of the club. Molyneux would keep that role until 1901 when he stood down after being asked to devote all his time to administration. He started well, with four wins from the initial five fixtures – his team hit 13 goals in those games. On 2 December 1889, at Anfield, Stoke (the club did not gain the appendage 'City' until 1925) were beaten 8–0, a League record at the time. In early January, Aston Villa were defeated 7–0, making Anfield feel like Goalville, Liverpool 4. That season, only Preston, who would go on to be crowned League

Champions, were to beat Everton on their own turf. That defeat was avenged when the Anfield lads became one of just two clubs to win (2-1) at Deepdale that campaign.

The FA Cup brought Derby County to Anfield on 18 January 1890 and 10,000 witnessed an historic match. The pitch was not in good condition, very heavy and with hardly any grass. Derby took an early 2-1 lead but Everton came out for the second half 3-2 up. The home side quickly added two more to their total and the heads of the County players seemed to fall as the state of the pitch began to deteriorate further. The match concluded with Everton winning 11-2, a result never matched by the club. Brady, Geary and Milward all scored hat-tricks (another club record). But the Cup glory was ended in the next round with a 4-2 defeat at the hands of Stoke.

At the end of the season, Everton were runners-up to Preston North End, with just a two-point gap between them. With 65 goals from 22 fixtures, previous problems with goal-scoring seemed to have been addressed. The pre-season signing of Fred Geary had done much to help as he was the club's top scorer, hitting 21 in 18 outings.

ANFIELD RISING

The gate receipts at Anfield for 1889/90 amounted to £5,188 5s 10d and, with the players' wages and other costs adding up to £2,059 1s 11d, Everton were clearly a profitable concern and a club with a growing fan base.

Everton started the 1890/91 term winning half-a-dozen and drawing one of their initial seven games. Fred Geary was the star of the early season, scoring 11 times as the team notched up 27 goals.

The next five League games saw four defeats for Everton. This disappointing run was followed by seven victories from eight fixtures. Everton went into their final two League matches with a four-point lead, needing just a draw in one of them to claim the Championship.

The last but one game was at Anfield against Preston North End, Everton's rivals for League glory. Around 15,000 witnessed Preston's 1–0 victory (so completing the double over the home side).

Now it was Burnley vs. Everton and Sunderland vs. Preston that would decide the Championship. Snow, sleet, an extremely slippery surface and 8,000 Burnley fans awaited Everton at Turf Moor (the crowd was swollen considerably by approximately 2,000 visiting supporters).

Sustained first-half pressure from Everton was to no avail and the players went into the break with a goalless 45 minutes behind them. After the interval, the home side, against the run of play, took the lead. However, Geary equalised within two minutes and on the hour an own goal put Everton ahead. Nerves seemed to take over as the away team became aware that the Championship was theirs for the taking and, seemingly as a consequence, with five minutes left to play, Burnley made it 2-2. But the draw would have been sufficient for Everton to take the title. However, Burnley's winning goal seemed to kill the collective hope of the city of Liverpool.

Despondency was changed to elation later in the day when the news broke that Preston had been defeated 3-0 at Sunderland giving Everton (and Liverpool) their first League title by a two-point margin from Preston (reversing the situation of the previous season). The Anfield side had hit 63 goals, three players scoring 42 of these; Geary got 20, Milward 12 and Chadwick 10. In the course of the season, the club had become the first to achieve a five-figure average attendance for home games (11,875).

ANFIELD RISING

Two advances were introduced to football during the 1890/91 season. In January 1891, the Football Association unveiled 'goal nets', which had been invented by Liverpool-born John Alexander Brodie, although legend has it that a Birmingham man had the original idea and that Brodie was motivated by Bob Lythgoe, who had been a goalkeeper for Liverpool Ramblers. Brodie worked in the engineering department of the Mersey Docks Estate. Although a former player and subsequent follower of rugby, he was inspired after seeing the difficulties that football referees had while watching a game at Anfield. Nets were initially deployed at the Liverpool Ramblers ground and the first League club to use them were Bolton Wanderers (oddly only at one end) in a game against Notts Forest on New Year's Day 1891. The then Pike's Lane-based side paid Mr Brodie (who had patented the idea) sixpence for the privilege of using his creation.

The first high-status game to see the use of nets was the North vs. South match of January 1891. However, it was some time before nets were deployed by every club as the FA wanted to pay what they saw as a fair price for the right to use

Brodie's invention. Ultimately, the sum of £3 12s 6d was agreed. Rigging was first seen in a Cup Final at the Oval in 1892, when West Bromwich Albion met Aston Villa (this last Kennington Final was won by Albion with goals from Alf Geddes, Sam Nicholls and John Reynolds). Strangely, nets are not compulsory in the modern laws of the game, but are included as a requirement in nearly every set of competition rules.

Penalty kicks were also introduced that season based on the idea of William McCrum ('Spot-kick Billy'), from Milford, County Armagh. The Irish Football Association presented the notion to the International Football Association Board and, following extended discussions, the board approved the penalty kick on 2 June 1891.

There were also developments off the pitch. In April 1890, the Liverpool dock workers had finally won the half-day Saturday after months of strikes and lock-outs. This had been a long fight for all workers, attested to by a letter to the *Liverpool Mercury* of July 1853: 'And why should not we also get some little time for recreation? Here have I been in an office for six years and never had but three days holiday, with the exception of Sundays.'

Hours in the docks were long and hard. Even the clerks would start work at 7 a.m. and toil through to 6 p.m. six days a week, although they were granted half a day off on a Saturday a full 22 years before the dock labourers. The struggle for the Saturday half-day had been particularly hard for dock workers who were employed on a casual basis. The impetus for the five-and-a-half-day working week was energised by the 'Nine Hours Movement' in the 1870s, and, by 1872, most skilled workers were entitled to have a day off on Saturdays.

Now, with much of the working class gaining free time on a Saturday afternoon, there was suddenly more time for leisure activities and the profit factor would start to play a part in mass-spectator sport. In Liverpool, the dockers' half-day freed up thousands of men to attend football in the afternoon, which would prove a tremendous boost for the game locally.

9

THE PARTING OF
THE WAYS

Everton's achievement of fifth place in the League in 1891/92 and some notable matches (not least a remarkable 4–3 win at Villa Park) were overshadowed by the momentous events off the field of play that season.

There were plenty of people still involved with the club that had been connected with it since it was a church side, playing in the local park. They had seen Everton rise from their original lowly status, move away from municipal grounds and push aside amateurism to take a place among the football elite of England in the relatively short period of 10 years. John Houlding had of course been central to all this. He had guided the club to Anfield, supplied the finance that enabled the construction of its stands, and led Everton into the Football League.

Houlding had overseen the occupation of Joseph Orrell's field at (initially) a relatively modest cost and Everton had enjoyed practically unfettered operation at Anfield, so maximising profit, a crucial necessity at that point in time. Orrell's leasing of the land to Everton has been described as 'an act of municipal altruism', although this is perhaps a tad naive. From the start it would have been understood that any success the team achieved could be reflected in the rent and if the side failed then they could always be evicted. Orrell's action was one of simple speculation with minimal developmental costs, although there is no doubt that the football club benefited from it. But the actual situation was obscured by Houlding's role in matters. He increased the 'rent' even though ostensibly Orrell had not. However, this did not prevent Orrell from raising his rent to Houlding, who would be free to pass this on to the club. Houlding placed himself at the centre as the representative tenant and he was the individual who had his hand on the pulse of Everton's rise with a finger in at least two pies; the growing prosperity of the club and so the requisite increase in rent. He seemed to have reached an understanding with Orrell from before the move to Anfield, the ins and outs of which were probably more complex than will ever be known.

The strength of feeling against Houlding's position was now at boiling point. The initial (1885/86) annual payment for the use of Anfield was £100; by 1888 this had risen to £240. The following year this had gone up again to £250. Houlding also insisted on having a nominee on the club's executive, thereby ensuring that someone would support his interests.

For some years there had been club members, some having continued links with St Domingo's Church, who didn't approve of the links with brewer- and pub-owning Houlding. But, as the 1890s began, there was a feeling that his power over the club seemed to know no bounds. Many saw him as taking advantage of his position and almost ruthless profiteering.

There is no denying that Houlding was playing his entrepreneurial role to its fullest extent, but in doing so he was merely replicating what others were doing in football at the time and would do in the future. The self-made Houlding was a man of

his time who was shaped by his background. He
would bring Liverpool Football Club into being on
the cusp of a vibrant, young 20th century, in the
port city of Liverpool, a growing, powerful and
wealthy metropolis. Houlding, like Gus Mears at
Chelsea a few years later, was a confirmed
capitalist, who believed that good business was
the basis of a healthy and wealthy society and,
despite his undoubted enthusiasm for football,
there is little to suggest that he would go into any
deal without the potential for profit.

Looking to bankroll League football, Everton's
finances were under strain and no one could
predict that Houlding would not put up the
rent even further. League football had seen
crowds rise by around 500 per cent since
Everton's first few seasons and Anfield had
grown to meet this demand.

At a general meeting on 15 September 1891 at
the Royal Street Hall, not far from Everton Valley,
Houlding supporter William E Barclay, the former
club secretary, took the chair. After reading some
letters from Orrell's solicitor, Houlding told of his
plan for the formation of a limited liability
company. A prepared printed prospectus proposed

the acquisition of Orrell's and Houlding's land, the stands, offices, etc., for a total of £9,237 10s.

Orrell had demanded an increase in rent for the ground and threatened to withdraw the tenancy unless certain alterations were carried out. There is no record or any kind of proof that Orrell and Houlding were working in tandem, and the Everton president's plan was ostensibly a counter to Orrell's position, which on the face of it seemed a good idea. But it became apparent that Houlding had bought land adjoining Anfield (that had been the property of the other Orrell brother) and this was included in the purchase plan. As such, he stood to make a considerable gain from the transaction he was recommending. Despite Houlding's earlier rejection of the proposed limited liability company, such a move now might have suited his purpose: the club would be able to buy the land he had purchased from Orrell and he could realise his investment. But it is also possible that Houlding sensed that he would not be able to hold out much longer against those who wished to oust him and that this proposal was his last effort to save what he could from the situation. He naturally did not want to be left with a football ground without a football team.

After taking questions, Barclay proposed and Mr Howarth seconded a resolution: 'That the scheme as explained be adopted.'

At this point, George Mahon, now a church elder and one of Liverpool's most senior and successful accountants, proposed an amendment, seconded by Mr Montgomery. This amounted to a rejection of Houlding's proposals and a request for the committee to take authority from the meeting to negotiate with Houlding about 'renting of such further land as may be required', subject to Houlding making the necessary arrangements with Orrell. Mahon's amendment was carried.

A series of executive meetings followed but no progress was made. Houlding wrote to the committee to bring their attention to the existing conditions of tenancy. In an effort to short-circuit the mounting pressure for the club to cut their losses and move, Houlding informed the committee that he would not give any undertaking about the stands. This meant that he would not guarantee to allow any attempt to relocate parts of or fittings from these structures and as such obstructed any ambitions to move to a new venue. However, it seems that this attitude in fact motivated the Mahon camp further.

A smart man with a well-kept beard, Mahon was an articulate person and, on 25 January 1892, during a special general meeting, at the College, Shaw Street, it was again stated that Houlding's plans for a limited liability company would not be accepted. This practically ensured that the club would not be able to stay at Anfield, as Orrell had determined to put up the rent, and Mahon led his supporters to Goodison Park, or the Mere Green Field as it was known at that time, on the other side of Stanley Park. In effect, Mahon had called Houlding's bluff.

Everton had offered Houlding £180 per annum but no reply was received and, as the club had been given notice to quit Anfield by Orrell, the club's solicitors were instructed to arrange for a lease of the ground in Goodison Road. The club would be formed into a limited company (this would allow funds to be raised for a ground move) under the name of the Everton Football Club Limited, with a capital of £500 in £1 shares, each member to be allowed one share.

Houlding, knowing that a football ground with no football club was something of a liability, recruited a group of individuals who had stayed loyal to Anfield and at a meeting held at Houlding's house William Barclay suggested that Everton would be entitled to retain their name and so a new club should be formed and called Liverpool Football Club. This demonstrated the ambition to have city-wide appeal (rather than to draw just specifically on the Everton district for support).

(Of course, in 1894, the club adopted the city's official red and yellow colours (in their first few seasons Liverpool wore blue and white halved jerseys, Everton at the time were sporting various stripes with red in them). The Anfield side incorporated the Liverbird within the club's emblem in 1901.)

But Houlding made it clear that he wanted Everton Football Club to continue to play at Anfield; he had registered a new company in Somerset House with the title of The Everton Football Club and Athletic Ground Company Limited. The signatures appended were Robert Berry, William (not John) Houlding, Alexander Nisbet, John James Ramsey, John Dermot, William Francis Evans and John McKenna.

The registration had been made without the full knowledge of the Everton committee members and as such Mahon pledged that his committee would work to protect the interests of the majority of members; according to FA and Football League rules, there could not be two Evertons. However, what this demonstrates is that a new Everton in fact left the old Everton and as such the Anfield club were the original institution; the second Everton 'emerged' from Anfield.

A hearing was held in London at the Football Association's headquarters. The FA Council adopted the following resolution: 'The Council, in accordance with its past decisions, will not accept any membership of any club bearing a name similar to one already affiliated with this Association in the name of the Everton club, and will only recognise the action of a majority of its members at a duly constituted meeting.'

So it was that Barclay's suggestion about the new club's name became reality. But, despite the enforced adoption of a new name, Liverpool were the predecessors of Everton (and not the other way round); there were, for a moment, two Evertons – the one that departed their erstwhile parent institution won an argument about a name, which in more litigious, less magnanimous, contemporary times might have been a much more hard-fought battle that could have gone the other way.

At an Everton committee meeting in February 1892, the resignations of Houlding, Barclay and Williams were accepted. During a meeting on Tuesday, 15 March 1892, the Everton president (Houlding) was effectively dismissed. The *Liverpool Review* wrote,

'King Houlding' of Everton has been ... kicked out of the presidency and from the committee of the Everton Football Club ... Years ago 'King Houlding' advanced the then struggling but rising Everton Football Club funds at a small rate of interest. He also assisted the organisation in other ways, for which the members were righteously thankful. As a landlord he lent the club a ground at a moderate rental to play on. He advanced money to erect grand stands, and provide all the rest of the paraphernalia of a first-class football club ... As the club prospered, the rental of the ground increased, and the interest asked by the landlord for money advanced went up perceptibly. There were mumblings and grumblings, and finally the storm burst. 'King Houlding' insisted that he was in the right; the great majority of members insisted that he was in the wrong. The 'King' began to assert his power; his subjects broke out in open rebellion. Very soon it became a war to the knife.

Finally, the 'King' has been 'kicked' and the victorious host have elected to migrate to pastures new and a fresh field, where a heavy rental will cease from troubling and the footballists will be at rest.

This business is very sad, and, as a large number of onlookers think, very stupid. There can be no doubt that 'King Houlding' has done a very great deal for the Everton Football Club, and no doubt the club has done something for 'King Houlding'. But neither of the contending parties seem prepared to admit this ... it really is a pity that a man like 'King Houlding' should be mixed up in such an unseemly wrangle as that which has been going on in Everton football for months past.

Perhaps 'King Houlding' will run a new football club on the present Everton ground

(Anfield). If he does, the migrators to the new ground in Goodison Road will have a rival bad to beat. The two organisations may prove more beneficial or more hurtful to local football generally than the one organisation under the old order of things ... To use a football term, 'King Houlding' is palpably offside. The organisation on Tuesday night numbered some 500 members, and of these only eighteen or 20 stood by the 'King'. The king is dead; long live the king.

Mahon claimed the majority of the grass-roots support. Press reports suggested that the whole situation had political undertones. But the *Liverpool Review* was pretty clear about the underlying situation: 'The split is purely a business one. If not, why all the talk and twaddle about "King Houlding" reaping incalculable wealth from his hotel ... surely the game of football is not going to be prostituted as a means of selling XXX [an allusion to alcohol]. This would be kicking "offside" indeed.'

Exactly a century later, during their Centenary season, Liverpool were sponsored for the first time by Carlsberg, the world-famous brewery.

Houlding, the footballing brewer, might well have got some pleasure out of the irony.

In April, under FA arbitration, it was agreed that Everton would receive £250 compensation for the cost of Anfield's stands. But, although Houlding had held on to his ground, before it could be serviceable for a professional team it required a great deal of work, as, following the rent dispute, Everton members had removed many of the fittings of the ground, including fixtures such as the turnstiles.

The FA's ruling put an end to Houlding continuing to use the name 'Everton' for any team he put together at Anfield or elsewhere and he re-registered his club in May 1892 as the Liverpool Association Football Club and Athletic Grounds Company Limited (however, it wasn't until 3 June that a special resolution and the seal of approval by the Board of Trade took effect). Initially, there had been an objection from Liverpool Rugby Club about the title Liverpool Football Club, hence the addition of the word 'Association' to Barclay's original suggestion, although the FA ruled that the rugby club had no monopoly on the name.

Barclay volunteered to be Liverpool's honorary

secretary and applied successfully for affiliations to the Football Association, Lancashire Association and Liverpool Association. John Houlding was elected president of the new club (the same role he had taken with Everton) and in order to help provide players for Liverpool he loaned the club £500, interest-free and with no pressure for repayment; Liverpool Football Club were born.

Houlding audaciously wrote to the Football League applying for membership. This, together with the whole chronicle of the split, was met with general amazement as most people believed that a city the size of Liverpool would not be able to give adequate support (in terms of crowd attendance or playing talent) to keep two ambitious football teams operating in such close proximity to each other.

The Football League were not sympathetic to Liverpool's application and rejected Houlding's request. As such, Liverpool were obliged to put all their eggs in the Lancashire Association basket.

Houlding, in later years, reckoned the dispute had been provoked by the temperance members at the club, who had long opposed his association with brewing and public houses, and, although there may be some truth in that perception, those who relocated to Goodison knew that, in order to get the most from the club in terms of financial return, they had to acquire their own property to be free of Houlding's influence and gain autonomy over the destiny of Everton Football Club.

10

'McUNITED'

Ulsterman John McKenna was to be an influential committee member and very much a mover and shaker in the first important years of Liverpool Football Club. He was certainly one of the visionaries who paved the way for modern football.

Like Houlding, McKenna was a nouveau riche entrepreneur. He had arrived in Liverpool as a nine-year-old and started his working life running errands and working as a grocery delivery boy. Via a range of business enterprises, he amassed sizeable wealth. He was a good-looking man with a handsome if exaggerated moustache and had been a regular at Anfield, invariably cosseted in his plush velvet-collared overcoat and crowned with an expensive bowler hat. A one-time rugby player, he had an intelligent understanding of football and knew where quality players might be recruited from, having good contacts in Scotland, and Glasgow in particular, and specifically within that city's Irish population. McKenna was to become an authoritative and significant figure during the early years of Liverpool.

McKenna was a true football enthusiast and loved everything about the game. When John Houlding moved on from his presidential involvement in the club, McKenna took on the organisational leadership, and it is impossible to underestimate his influence on Liverpool's history during this period.

A thoughtful and intelligent person, he had uncommon powers of judgement and was among the game's most attractive personalities in the early days of Liverpool FC.

William E Barclay became Liverpool's first secretary-manager, continuing the role he had played at Everton, although he was never quite to get away from the notion that he was 'assistant secretary' to McKenna. McKenna performed most of what might be understood in more modern terms as the managerial duties at Anfield before Barclay was officially appointed to the staff of Liverpool FC (and after). Unusual for this time, Barclay liked to spend time with his players (most men in this role during that era left that sort of thing to trainers and remained more or less aloof). He was a capable organiser with a good network of contacts in the game and travelled all over the country in search of talent, which he had a good eye for. With McKenna, he brought many fine players to Anfield.

A respected and well-liked person across football and the city of Liverpool, Barclay made a success of most of the projects he was involved with; he was also a popular headmaster of the Industrial Schools (institutions intended to solve problems of juvenile delinquency by removing poor and neglected children from their home environment to a boarding school) in Everton Crescent. Barclay went on to be chairman and worked for the Football Association.

While Everton were playing out their debut at Goodison (a friendly vs. Bolton Wanderers) on the evening of Thursday, 1 September 1892, Liverpool

Football Club also contested their first match, also a friendly against Rotherham Town at Anfield.

The Liverpool directors had boldly forecasted a good start, and the *Liverpool Echo* reported, 'The old Anfield ground will be occupied by the newly organised club known as the Liverpool Association and the officials claim for it that no better game will be witnessed on any of the plots in the neighbourhood.'

Everton achieved a comfortable 4–2 victory but Liverpool hit the Midland Leaguers for seven while the Yorkshiremen had just a single reply. According to the *Liverpool Daily Post*'s first ever Liverpool match report, 'Amidst applause Councillor J. Houlding started the ball.'

The Liverpool line-up was: Ross, Hannah (captain), McLean, Kelso, McQueen, McBride, Wyllie, Smith, Miller, McVean, Kelvin.

Hannah won the toss and early in the first half McVean scored the first goal in the history of Liverpool Football Club. Kelvin and Wyllie quickly added to the home team's account and at half-time Hannah and his men were five goals up.

The *Liverpool Echo* optimistically predicted a few days later, 'It is much to be feared that they will win most of their engagements in the same easy fashion.'

As the *Book of Football* (1906) told, 'The "gates" were poor.' In fact, there had been just a handful of spectators to watch Liverpool's opening game and the club were unable to meet their visitors' financial guarantee (a fee agreed for visiting teams playing friendlies); Goodison had been packed out with a crowd of 10,000.

The fruits of McKenna's recruitment journey North of the border meant that there was not a single Englishman in that first Liverpool side and on paper it looked more like 'McUnited' (the Irishman had recruited 13 men to the Anfield cause, eight of whom had names with the prefix 'Mc'); Duncan McClean and John McBride had been drawn from Renton, the West Dunbartonshire side who were the first club to lay claim to the title Champions of the World, after, in 1888, as Scottish Cup holders, they defeated the FA Cup winners West Bromwich Albion. Malcolm McVean had joined from Third Lanark, the Scottish Cup winners of 1889 (and finalists in 1876 and 1878; in 1904 the Thirds would be Scottish Champions). This powerful quartet linked up with Hugh

McQueen, Matt McQueen, John McCartney, Bill McOwen and Joe McQue. Some idea of the kind of payment players could command at this time is demonstrated by an ex-Celtic forward at the start of the 1893/94 season offering his services to Liverpool for £8 down, £3 a week and £1 5s (£1.25) during the close season.

(In 1986, Liverpool made sure of the FA Cup/League Championship Double with a team devoid of Englishmen – although Steve McMahon was named as substitute in the Cup Final side, he didn't play – but there were only four Scots in that team.)

On the following Saturday, Liverpool contested their second game, once more at Anfield, for their initial Lancashire League fixture. Their opponents, Higher Walton, were the Champions of 1889/90 but it was Liverpool who were the winners that day. When Walton finally got to Anfield three-quarters-of-an-hour late, the home side, led by skipper McVean, hit eight goals while not allowing the visitors much more than a sniff of a chance.

Only 200 people had turned up to witness the victory, but, within the week, Liverpool's early glory had become hot gossip all over the city and on 24 September there were 4,000 at Anfield to watch Liverpool beat Bury 4–0.

Liverpool's debut campaign in the Lancashire League, meeting clubs such as Blackpool and Bury, could hardly have gone better; they had played 22 games, won 17 and lost just three, scoring 66 goals (an average of exactly three each match) while conceding just 19 (less than one a game), and they topped the table on goal average.

During the initial rounds of the Liverpool Senior Cup, the Liverpool FA did what they could to prevent Liverpool and Everton being drawn against each other in the early rounds. Liverpool defeated Bootle 1–0 at Anfield in the last four and this set up a clash with their near neighbours. At a meeting convened in the Neptune Hotel on the evening after the semi-final, the Cup committee agreed that the Final would be staged the following Saturday at Bootle, with the game scheduled to start at 4 p.m.

In the days before the Final, there was a rumour that both clubs would not send out full-strength sides. It was felt that Everton, having close to 30 top-class players on their books, wanted to give second-string men a chance to win something and, in fact, Everton organised a game at short notice against the fine Scottish side Renton at Goodison Park (which ended in a 1–1 draw) for the same afternoon as the Final.

The very first Merseyside derby took place on 22 April 1893. The break-up was of course still fresh in the memory, and as such the anticipated highly competitive encounter was laden with animosity.

The friendly against Renton hardly affected the attendance at the Liverpool Senior Cup Final as a crowd of 10,000 packed Bootle's Hawthorne Road ground. As the players came out (of what would later be the cricket pavilion), it became clear that the Everton team were made up of players from both the first team and the reserve side; however, just four of the Everton XI had made double figures for League appearances that term (Everton had played 30 League games in Division One the previous season). The Blues line-up (with League outings detailed) was: Williams (11), A Chadwick (3), Collins (9), Boyle (25), Holt (26), Coyle (0), Gordon (11), Murray (3), Hartley (1), McMillan (2), Elliott (captain, 2).

However, Liverpool fielded their best XI and as such looked a much stronger unit in terms of League outings (at this time Liverpool were not members of the Football League, so the figures represent the number of Lancashire League games they played the previous season out of a possible 22): McOwen (1), Hannah (captain, 22), McLean (22), McCartney (18), McQue (18), McBride (20), Wyllie (22), McVean (21), Miller (21), M McQueen (16), H McQueen (16).

Liverpool, by way of Miller, kicked off, playing into the sun while Everton were obliged to run into a strong wind.

It was a tough tackling war from the start, but the referee, Blackburn Rovers man and seven-times England international Herbie Arthur, seemingly wanted to keep the flow going and let much pass as the proverbial six of one and half-a-dozen of the other.

With little more than 30 minutes played, Liverpool took the lead after Miller gained possession and passed to Wyllie, who reacted swiftly with a shallow drive that surprised the Everton keeper Williams. Everton's response was to up the aggression level in the tackle; Liverpool countered in kind and the referee felt obliged to act, lecturing McQue at length.

The half-time break was extended to give the

players a chance to recover from the effects of the hot conditions. Not long after the whistle signalled the start of the second half, Gordon laid on a simple chance for McMillan, but his head didn't connect well enough to cause a problem.

A breakaway by Liverpool forced Williams to rush forward to cover the danger. Arthur was animated with his whistle as the free-kick total grew apace, and from one of these Liverpool looked to have doubled their lead. But the seeming goal was disallowed.

The pressure seemed to exert itself on both teams, no better demonstrated by the forced separation of McQue and Murray. The crowd were now in full roar as Everton began to dominate and a desperate-looking Liverpool were happy to punt the ball out of play at every opportunity.

In the dying moments of the game, Everton were awarded a corner. As the ball fell, it looked to some as if a Liverpool defender had punched it away and the Everton players appealed furiously for the penalty. The referee consulted his linesman (who had only replaced umpires two years earlier) and awarded a drop-ball, but as this was being enacted Arthur blew to signal full-time.

Huge tumult followed, in which Everton were quick to lodge a protest against the result, complaining about 'the general incompetence of the referee'.

The remonstration meant that Liverpool could not be presented with the trophy straight after the game. The Liverpool FA felt obliged to call a meeting at the Neptune Hotel for the following Monday to debate issues arising from the Final. But Everton's appeal was thrown out, and, following Liverpool's match with Preston North End at Anfield on the Tuesday, the Liverpool Senior Cup was presented by Mr AB Hull, the Liverpool FA president, who congratulated Liverpool on their win against Everton and their successful first season in the Lancashire League. John Houlding replied by saying he was happy 'to welcome the piece of plate back as an old friend'.

This was understood to be a reference to Everton's previous successes in the Liverpool Senior Cup, when Houlding was with them; Everton had won that trophy six times in its 10-year history and had retained it for three seasons prior to Liverpool's first win.

The Liverpool players received gold 'Bovril'

medals (thus demonstrating an early example of football sponsorship/product placement).

The Anfield men fought their way though two qualifying rounds of the Lancashire Senior Cup, defeating Southport and West Manchester to meet Darwen in the first round proper. A 1–0 win set up a meeting with Bootle in front of 5,000 rabid Bucks supporters and the visitors were defeated 2–1.

In the FA Cup first qualifying round, Liverpool were drawn against Nantwich at Jackson Avenue. There were no goals by half-time but in the end the Dabbers were beaten 4–0 with Miller getting a hat-trick. The next qualifying round brought Newton to Anfield to be destroyed 9–0. But at the Drill Field, it was 2–1 after the first 45 minutes and, with the score remaining unchanged by the final whistle, Northwich Victoria ended Liverpool's creditable first-season run.

With 29 goals in three competitions, former Dunbarton man John Miller was easily Liverpool's top marksman.

The scandal of the season happened when both Liverpool's newly acquired trophies were stolen. The club were obliged to replace the lost cups, which cost the fledgling side a huge (for the time) £127 for the new trophies. This was quite a blow as, despite the club's runaway success and the fact that away from home Liverpool could pull crowds close to 8,000 regularly, Anfield was simply not attracting the punters, for the most part drawing at best half that figure (although the Lancashire Senior Cup third qualifying round game vs. Darwen drew 8,000 to Anfield).

It was clear that something needed to be done; Liverpool had to be perceived as at least equal in status to their already bitter rivals Everton. McKenna saw a window of opportunity offered by something of a triple whammy: Accrington (one of the original 12 founder members of the Football League) declined to take up a Second Division place following their relegation from Division One; the Football League decided at the conclusion of the 1892/93 term to expand Division Two (in its second season) by adding three clubs to the existing dozen; and Bootle (the first winners of the Liverpool Senior Cup in 1883), despite finishing in eighth place, resigned from the League. McKenna resolved, without consulting or even telling a soul, to telegraph the Football

League. His message was short and sweet: 'Liverpool make application to the Second Division of the League.'

This was a rare opportunity to go for one of five vacancies for entry into the Football League. Rotherham Town and Newcastle United were given membership without a vote being taken; Liverpool, Woolwich Arsenal and Middlesbrough Ironopolis (a professional splinter team from Middlesbrough Football Club that were formed in 1889 but would be dissolved in 1894 when they lost their Paradise Ground home) were elected at a subsequent meeting. There were just two other candidates recorded, Loughborough Town and Doncaster Rovers (Doncaster would have to wait until 1901 for election).

Liverpool (with 18 votes), Newcastle (4 votes) and Arsenal (13 votes) between them would be England's top club an amazing 35 times up to 2008.

Bootle, a local side, had pushed themselves to the forefront of football through an energetic recruiting policy, drawing Welshmen from the famous Druids of Ruabon as well as players from Essex and from all over Lancashire during an era when there was no formal transfer system. Local rivalry was intense but perhaps the club had been over-ambitious during their single season in the League. It was recorded that the directors had spent £120 but had got little support in return for their expense and were thus beset with financial problems.

Bootle, who actually delayed their final decision on resignation to the opening day of the season, had a distinguished history, and had earned the nickname 'Brutal Bootle' in recognition of their attitude to the game.

In the background, Barclay had been opposed to Liverpool joining the League. He had known nothing of McKenna's initial application, only finding out when he was handed a telegram from the Football League which was almost as succinct as McKenna's submission had been; it read, 'Liverpool elected. Come to London at 3pm tomorrow to arrange fixtures.'

11
FOOTBALL
LEAGUE
LIVERPOOL

Liverpool Football Club played their debut match in the Football League on 2 September 1893 at the Paradise Ground against Middlesbrough Ironopolis. A 'large and enthusiastic crowd' (it was about 2,500) turned up to witness the event on what was a bright, sunny day.

The game started at a furious pace and in the first minutes both keepers were obliged to earn their pay, each making notable saves. The long grass wasn't helping Liverpool's precise, low-passing style. However, the visitors' pressure seemed to be paying off when Stott drilled a shallow drive that went close. Hugh McQueen struck an upright a few minutes later.

Miller looked threatening, bearing down on the Liverpool goal, but McLean's tackle was perfectly timed and denied the Ironopolis centre-forward any chance of making good his attack. A chance for Liverpool's Gordon was swiftly followed by an equally ominous Ironopolis effort that almost allowed Cooper to put the home side in front.

Early in the second half, Henderson messed up a simple opportunity following Stott's fine pass. After this, Liverpool poured forward and shots from Hugh McQueen and Gordon both went just the wrong side of the posts.

It seemed that it would only be a matter of time before Ironopolis succumbed to what had become the consistent pressure of the Liverpool attack and it was Malcolm McVean who, after over an hour, scored Liverpool's debut goal in the Football League.

Just minutes later, a thunderous shot from Gordon left Nixon helpless, but his work, seemingly unjustly, was ruled offside.

To their credit, in spite of the sustained assault they were experiencing, Ironopolis continued to look for any chance to press forward to seek the equalising goal. But this commitment had the cost of leaving their defence exposed and Joe McQue was the man to take advantage of that situation with a searing 25-yard strike to put Liverpool 2–0 up, a situation that was not to change as the home side struggled to hold off their visitors.

The teams that day were:

MIDDLESBROUGH IRONOPOLIS: Nixon; Upton, Adams, McNair, Mackie, Garbut, Allport, Hunter, Miller, Cooper, Deactin

LIVERPOOL: McOwen; Hannah, McLean, Henderson, McQue, McBride, Gordon, McVean, M McQueen, Stott, H McQueen

On 9 September 1893, Anfield staged its first Football League game and there were 5,000 present to witness Lincoln City being well beaten. Jim McBride, after 16 minutes, got the first of his two goals (and the first Liverpool League goals at Anfield) in the 4–0 victory. Liverpool completed the double over Ironopolis at Anfield with an unforgiving 6–0 scoreline at the start of October and in their first seven games they had amassed 13 points from a possible 14 (only being denied a perfect record by a 1–1 draw at Trent Bridge).

On 28 October, Liverpool travelled to Plumstead, South London, to meet Woolwich Arsenal. Having won the toss, the visitors gained the advantage of having the strong wind behind them. The first half-hour was a swift and even contest before Liverpool were awarded a free-kick about 50 yards from the Woolwich goal. McCartney placed the ball skilfully but, although Williams made contact with a leg, the ball ricocheted into the net. The wind and Liverpool gaining the lead seemed to cause the home side's collective head to drop. Matt McQueen's lengthy, hard punt from the middle of the field, buoyed by the wind, sailed into the top of the Arsenal goal. Soon after, a similar effort from Hugh McQueen (Matt's younger brother) put Arsenal further in the red. Coming out of something of a scrum, Stott scored the Scousers' fourth goal. Seemingly encouraged by his work for the third goal of the game, Hugh McQueen claimed his second, again from way out.

With just the first 45 minutes played, the visitors were 5–0 ahead. So, when Maidstone man Mr Craven blew for the start of the second period, the 7,000 Manor Ground faithful feared the worst. But the home side had decided to up the physical side of their play and, as Liverpool replied in kind, it all became a bit 'confrontational'. At one point, Mr Craven lectured Bradshaw for purposefully putting the boot into Buist with no pretence of an effort to play the ball. The crowd called for Bradshaw to be sent off, but he continued to work away at the Arsenal attack.

The game fragmented into a series of nasty scraps, but close to the final whistle Williams was called upon to make a number of fine saves as Liverpool went looking for yet more blood.

The line-ups were:

WOOLWICH ARSENAL: Williams; Powell, Storrs, Crawford, Buist, Howat, Shaw, Henderson, Heath, Elliott, Booth

LIVERPOOL: McOwen; Hannah, McLean, McCartney, M McQueen, McBride, Dick, McVean, Bradshaw, Stott, H McQueen

This form was indicative of the Anfield men's campaign. By the conclusion of their first Division Two schedule, Liverpool were undefeated over their 28 fixtures. In 22 victories and six draws, they hit the rigging 77 times, letting in just 18. Liverpool easily won the League, eight points above Birmingham City, but this was a time when there was no such thing as automatic promotion and Liverpool had to face a Test Match with Newton Heath (the club that would evolve into Manchester United) who had finished at the foot of Division One. The Heathens were defeated 2–0 at Ewood Park and Liverpool claimed a place in the top flight, a truly magnificent achievement.

Liverpool had entered the FA Cup in the first round proper, starting out with a 3–0 Anfield win against Grimsby. This was followed by a fine victory over First Division Preston North End, semi-finalists of the previous year, Liverpool getting three of the five goals scored in front of 18,000 Anfield supporters. But Bolton on their own turf, cheered on by 20,000 Trotters fans, were too much for the travelling Scousers; 2–0 down at half-time, Liverpool made their way back to Merseyside having shipped three goals without finding an answer.

It was a much better performance by Liverpool than it looked as Bolton got to the Final where they met Notts County at Goodison Park. County won 4–1, with goals by James Logan (3) and Arthur Watson. Jim Cassidy netted for Bolton.

With 14 goals to his credit, Darlington-born Jim Stott was Liverpool's sharpest shooter of the term, with Hugh McQueen bagging 11.

Liverpool started the new season, their first in the top flight of the English game, with two draws before Aston Villa put an end to their undefeated run of 31 games, which was to stand as a Football League record for many years. The First Division was to be a demanding environment for the young club; with nine games played, they were without a win, having lost five.

The Liverpool derby is the oldest top-flight, and perhaps the most hotly contested, derby in English football, and the inaugural all-Merseyside Football League encounter took place at Goodison Park on 13 October 1894. Liverpool, desperate to do well, went into special training for a week at Hightown, although Everton did nothing out of the ordinary. The *Liverpool Echo* called the game the 'great football match'.

Before the main game started, the 44,000 crowd (a League record at the time), which included the

Lord Mayor and other representatives of the great and the good of the city, watched a schoolboy contest between Liverpool and Nottingham that was in sharp contrast to the war that followed. Liverpool's play was ruthless and showed scant regard for their more graceful neighbours. It was an exciting exhibition, and the divergent styles of the neighbours made for a fascinating confrontation: Liverpool with their 'kick and run' strategy and notorious tough attitude, Everton offering a more genteel approach. At first Everton were overwhelmed by Liverpool's shock and awe tactics but it was McInnes who opened the scoring with a well-timed header to give Everton the advantage at half-time. In the second half, Latta and Bell put the match beyond the visitors and Everton were the 3–0 winners. However, Bradshaw had missed an easy chance for Liverpool that might have changed the whole character of the match. (On 20 February 1897, Henry (Harry) Bradshaw would become Liverpool's first full international player when he was selected for England against Ireland; the game attracted 14,000 to Trent Bridge, Nottingham. With the great Steve Bloomer getting two goals, Charlie Athersmith netting a single and George Wheldon claiming a hat-trick, the English stormed to a 6–0 victory.)

On 17 November, the draw with Everton pulled in 30,000. Jimmy Ross, Liverpool's 'Little Demon', scored a last-minute penalty equaliser (over the next two seasons Ross would hit 37 goals in 73 games) to make the derby game a four-goal thriller.

Before New Year, Liverpool had won just two matches and lost 11 of their 20 fixtures. Plagued by injuries throughout what was a harsh winter, Liverpool struggled on difficult and often dangerous pitches. When the season concluded, their record showed that they had only seven wins to their credit and had lost half of their 30 fixtures. This meant facing Bury in a promotion/relegation Test Match played at Ewood Park. Despite the Bury goalkeeper being sent off, Liverpool lost the game 1–0 and they were thus relegated.

Liverpool's short initial stay in the First Division was more the result of luck than innate inability of the club's players. The injury list made long and difficult reading for most of the season and the club had been unable to field the same team in consecutive games.

The FA Cup saw Liverpool defeat Barnsley St

Peter's twice to make it through to the next round. At Barnsley they won 2–1, Ross scoring the winner in extra-time.

According to the *Liverpool Daily Post*, 'At the close of the game, the Barnsley officials laid a protest with the referee in accordance with Rule 17 which provides that extra-time can only be ordered if both clubs mutually consent. Prior to extra-time being started, Barnsley protested and evidently the match will have to be counted as a draw and replayed at Liverpool.'

At Anfield, Barnsley were comprehensively beaten 4–0, but Liverpool's hopes in the Cup were dashed by Nottingham Forest at Anfield in the following round. Two goals in the first half were enough to see off the home side.

Over the season, Tom Bradshaw had hit 18 goals but, with Ross being the only other player to get into double figures (13), Liverpool were clearly lacking firepower.

According to the *Book of Football*, 'It is combination rather than individual excellence that wins League matches. One "star" among ten "sticks" is no use except for stage purposes.'

No one at Liverpool would have argued with

that. But a club also needs supporters and at points 'there were not enough spectators to go round the field' at Anfield.

John McKenna promised that Liverpool's sojourn in the Second Division would not be a protracted one and that the side would bounce straight back into the elite.

McKenna went back to Scotland to recruit a new set of mercenaries, one of whom was George Allan, from Leith Athletic. (The young centre-forward would become the club's first Scottish international when he played for his country against England on 3 April 1897 at Crystal Palace. With goals from Tom Hyslop in the 27th minute and Jimmy Millar seven minutes from time, Allan and his team claimed a fine 2–1 victory. Tragically, George was to pass away before his 25th birthday.)

Archie Goldie was another McKenna capture from Clyde and Frank Becton, who came from Preston North End, arrived at Anfield in the spring of 1895. Goldie was to be an inspiration in defence, while Becton and Allan would stack up the goals alongside Jimmy Ross, also a Deepdale import.

There were whispers of covert attempts to poach Liverpool's best players but the new president, William Houlding (John's son), worked with McKenna and his committee to hold on to all the club's players.

Anfield lagged behind the facilities at Goodison Park, so, demonstrating the club's determination and intentions, a new main stand was built that could house 3,000 fans. This major improvement of the ground cost £1,000 and it was a good investment, which remained in use for three-quarters of a century; it was to be a well-known feature of football in England, and its red and white mock-Tudor style (similar to the main stand at St James' Park) with the club's name in the centre, topped by ornate ironwork, became an iconic symbol of the club. But it wasn't until 1906, when Liverpool won the League Championship for the second time, that the first 'Kop' was built.

12

BOUNCING
BACK

With 10 victories and four losses behind them, on 7 December 1895, Liverpool ran out to Anfield's lowest ever League attendance; just 1,000 people turned up for the 1–0 victory over Loughborough. But during the 1895/96 campaign Liverpool claimed 22 wins and lost only six games in the extended (16-club) Second Division. They dropped just one point at home (a goalless draw with Darwen). True to his word, McKenna had led his team to the Division Two Championship (on goal average from Manchester City) and, apart from a 2–0 defeat against West Bromwich Albion at Stoney Lane (Small Heath were their other opponents in the three-club, four home and away games contest), sailed through the Test Matches (taking five points from four games) to return to the Division One.

On 3 April, Allan scored Liverpool's 106th goal of the 1895/96 campaign. This was the first and last time the side bettered a century of League goals in the course of a single season. A big contribution to this tally had come during the Anfield meeting with Rotherham Town on 18 February 1896.

Around 2,000 supporters bewailed the luck of Jimmy Ross as his powerful early shot clipped off the Rotherham woodwork, but a short while later McVean hit the opening goal, scoring with a good drive, but one that Wilkinson probably should have saved.

McVean, getting on the end of a fine cross by Allan, doubled his account and his side's lead. But there was no let-up from the hosts and at the restart they once more claimed possession; Wilkie's pass was picked up by the impressive Allan and the Liverpool centre-forward, with just eight minutes played, claimed his club's third goal. But it seemed the home side were insatiable and Allan appeared among the most ravenous of the

Anfield men. He made the ball his on the edge of his own penalty area before sending Ross off on a stunning run which only concluded with his smashing home Liverpool's fourth; he had left a string of defenders in his wake.

Unbelievably, just 18 minutes had ticked by when McVean finished off a scintillating attack that had seen Bradshaw and Ross combine brilliantly.

There was no reprieve and the Rotherham goal continued to be peppered with the fruits of Liverpool assaults. Five minutes on from McVean's fifth, Ross tried a long shot; Wilkinson came at it with his fists but only assisted the ball into the net.

At around the half-hour mark, Storer touched the ball for the first time. The visitors had been rocked to the core and were glad to get off the field at half-time.

As the players came out for the second half, there was no sign that Liverpool had lost their appetite for the game (even if Rotherham had). But, after two more goals from Allan, Town managed to put together a rare attack and Cutts, with a simple shot, gave his side at least something to show for their trip.

However, after Becton scored from a corner,

Ross came steaming out of his own half on a dazzling run that Allan was to capitalise on, putting Liverpool into double figures and hitting his fourth goal of the game.

The teams were:

LIVERPOOL: Storer; Goldie, Wilkie, McCartney, McQue, Holmes, McVean, Ross, Allan, Becton, Bradshaw

ROTHERHAM TOWN: Wilkinson; Porteous, Broadhead, Longden, Doughtrey, Widdowson, Bryant, Webster, Cutts, Wheatcroft, Mattison

In the Cup, Millwall were beaten 4–1 at Anfield, but the trip to Wolves proved too much for Liverpool and the Molineux men were 2–0 victors. Wolves were to be the beaten finalists that year, losing a tight match at Crystal Palace to the Wednesday, 2–1.

George Allan claimed 29 goals, but Jim Ross ran him close for the title of the club's top marksman for most of the season and ended with 24 nets.

Liverpool's return to Division One, while not emphatically successful, was good enough to push them into a very respectable fifth place, having drawn twice with the Champions, Aston Villa, and finishing one point and two positions above Everton. Liverpool also made their first real mark in the FA Cup. After getting just the better of Burton Swifts in a seven-goal thriller, wins away at West Bromwich Albion (2–1) and Nottingham Forest (after a replay) followed, no easy route, given that West Brom and Forest were both fellow First Division clubs. This led to Liverpool's debut in the semi-finals of the Cup.

Drawn against Aston Villa, who would retain their League Championship title that term, Liverpool travelled to Bramall Lane. In the other semi-final Everton met Derby County at the Victoria Ground. For the first time a Merseyside Final was possible. Everton did their bit but Liverpool went down 3–0 in a game that the headline in the *Liverpool Football Echo* called 'AGONY FOR LIVERPOOL' which was 'watched with almost painful anxiety and interest'. It seemed that the week of training at St Anne's had not been enough to prepare Liverpool for the struggle against the strong winds and the dour Villans. According to the *Echo*, 'The Anfielders had lost all heart and were overplayed.'

Villa and Everton met at Crystal Palace and the Birmingham side won 3–2, with goals by John Campbell, Fred Wheldon and Jimmy Crabtree. Jack Bell and Richard Boyle were on target for Everton.

With results elsewhere going their way, Villa confirmed their status as League Champions on the same day as they won the Cup. This made them the only team to date to achieve the League and Cup Double on the same day.

Frank Becton was selected at inside left for the Football League against the Scottish League that season, playing at Goodison Park in front of a crowd of 16,000.

Liverpool were starting to be a footballing force to be reckoned with and for the next eight years would not be moved from the company of England's best.

In August 1896, perhaps feeling that his team needed something extra, John McKenna recruited Tom Watson, the secretary of Sunderland (the 'Team of all the Talents'), to act as the secretary-manager at Anfield. Watson has been described as one of football's first great managers and had led the Black Cats to three titles in the First Division. The lure of higher wages brought him to Anfield.

Over the next two dozen years, time and again, his appointment would prove to have been an astute move by McKenna. Watson brought a particular dynamic brand of professionalism to the character of Liverpool's teams. Like his predecessor Barclay, Watson has often been viewed, at least in his initial years at Anfield, as being little more than an assistant to the vibrant McKenna, but he was nevertheless a shrewd manager and signed some outstanding players, including the great goalkeepers Ted Doig, Elisha Scott and Sam Hardy, strikers Jack Parkinson and Sam Raybould and of course the remarkable, tough-tackling defender Alex Raisbeck (although it seems McKenna spotted this phenomenal goal-scoring forward).

Alex Raisbeck was the Reds' first star player; another Scot, he was one of seven mining brothers hailing from Polmont, a village in Stirlingshire. He had been with Edinburgh Hibernian and in 1897 had played for the Scottish League against the English League. He joined Stoke in the First Division but after just a handful of appearances returned to Scotland. However, he was spotted by John McKenna while he was with the Potters and the Irishman sent Tom Watson to Edinburgh to get

Raisbeck's signature; Alex was to play 340 games for the club over the next decade and had a leading role in Liverpool's establishment in English football. He gained his first full cap in April 1900 and went on to play seven games for his country, five times as captain. Arguably one of the best centre-halves of his time, the fair-haired Raisbeck was a belligerent competitor who went into the tackle with strength and commitment. Just 5' 9" tall, he nevertheless habitually out-jumped bigger opponents. Raisbeck was hugely popular at Anfield and his name continues to be ranked alongside great Liverpool Scots such as Liddell and Dalglish.

One of Watson's best signings was Everton's Billy Lacey. Bill came to Anfield in an exchange deal for two players who hadn't managed to command a first-team place. Another great move was Arthur Goddard, who made 415 appearances under Watson.

Liverpool's 1897/98 campaign was a pretty colourless series. The side finished just four points clear of the bottom two clubs in ninth place. Curiously, Liverpool had beaten Champions Sheffield United at Bramall Lane 2–1 just before New Year and lost to the Blades at Anfield 4–0 in February.

Having reached the third round of the FA Cup after a replay with Newton Heath, Liverpool were once more obliged to play two games, this time against Derby County, going down 5–1 at the Baseball Ground. The Rams went on to the Final where they met Nottingham Forest at Crystal Palace. Forest won 3–1, with goals from Arthur Capes (2) and John McPherson. Steve Bloomer got Derby's goal.

The season finished on a high and hopeful note at Anfield with a 4–0 victory over Aston Villa. With 13 goals, Frank Becton was Liverpool's best in front of goal. No one else broke double figures.

13

CLOSE BUT
NO CIGAR

Liverpool started to make a telling impact in 1899, looking a good bet for the Double (victory in the League and Cup) as the season matured. With three matches left of their League schedule, the Reds were sitting proudly at the top of the First Division; Aston Villa were second but with an inferior goal average. Liverpool beat Bury and Blackburn, scoring three without conceding, but Villa smashed home 13 goals, which, with one game left to play, put them fractionally ahead of the Anfield men. Everything depended on the last game of the season, Liverpool's trip to Villa Park. Both clubs had 43 points, but now Villa had the marginally better goal average. A crowd of 41,357 paid £1,500 (a record for a League game) to see the classic confrontation. At Anfield, on 29 April 1899, Liverpool had lost 3–0 to Villa who went two better on their home turf. The five goals were scored in the first 35 minutes and Liverpool, finding no reply, were obliged to satisfy themselves with bettering Everton by two places and five points to take the runners-up spot (and they had scored their first 'double' over Everton). But, having played 16 games in 43 days, Liverpool had looked exhausted for much of the match.

After creditable victories over Blackburn Rovers, Newcastle United and West Bromwich Albion, Liverpool had made the last four of the Cup for the second time in three seasons and were drawn to meet Sheffield United at Nottingham Forest's new City ground. The game was a tale of defensive errors and the victory was snatched from Liverpool in the dying moments of the match. The Merseysiders were leading 2–1 following confusion between the Blades' defender Thickett and his keeper Foulke, and Morgan took the opportunity to claim what was a soft goal from the Sheffield side's perspective. United had scored the opening goal when Storer was brought down by one of his own defenders trying to stop Hedley taking advantage of an open goal. Ernie Needham hit the last-gasp equaliser.

The replay was an even more feverish affair, reflected in the 4–4 scoreline after extra-time at Burden Park; Liverpool had twice led by two goals. The third encounter was the first FA Cup semi-final in history to be abandoned. The match took place on a Monday afternoon and at half-time Liverpool were 1–0 up, thanks to Allan, but, after the crowd constantly spilled on to the pitch of the totally inappropriate and overcrowded Fallowfield ground, Manchester, the light was fading fast; the first half had taken 105 minutes to play due to the time taken up getting people off of the field of play. The referee was left with no choice but to pronounce the match void. The ground, with its capacity of just 15,000, had been overwhelmed by the 30,000 who turned up.

The circus moved on to the Baseball Ground and it was Fred Priest who scored the only goal of the game five minutes from time to send Liverpool home disappointed. Five and three-quarter hours of football had been played, both sides hitting seven goals each. But Liverpool's seventh was a goal that never was and they had to wait 15 more years to get to their first Final.

George Allan and Hugh Morgan hit 10 goals each in the League but Allan got four in the FA Cup run to Morgan's three.

At Crystal Palace, 73,833 watched Final debutants the Blades hit four second-half goals – Bennett, Beers, Almond and Priest – in reply to Boag's 12th-minute effort that had given Derby County the lead.

At the start of the 1899/1900 season, Liverpool created an unenviable record by losing their first eight League games. They managed only 49 goals in all and finished in 10th place. John Walker and Tom Robertson tied as the top guns with just 10 goals each. Once more the side did better than Everton who, a point behind their neighbours, took 11th spot, although Everton had gained vengeance for the previous campaign, beating Liverpool on both sides of Stanley Park. Highlights of Liverpool's season included a 5-2 Anfield victory over Manchester City and an exciting 3-3 draw with Champions Aston Villa. The Cup held even less drama than the League for Liverpool. Stoke were beaten in an Anfield replay and, after

ANFIELD RISING

Liverpool drew 1–1 with West Bromwich Albion, the Baggies won the second-round replay 2–1.

The season had been disappointing given Liverpool's previous form, but things were about to change.

14

THE FIRST CHAMPIONSHIP

Liverpool started what was to be a remarkable season with few changes to the squad from the previous campaign. Right-back John Robertson, who had played in the Scottish Cup Final for Hibernian in 1896, came from Stoke in the close season and he proved an invaluable signing.

Liverpool's strength was the side's defensive play and the inspiration in this department was Alex Raisbeck. His hard tackling and fine heading ability together with his accurate passing made him the rock in the midst of the Anfield men.

The initial part of the season was mediocre for Liverpool. Things started well enough, with three consecutive victories and a draw at Goodison Park.

But a home defeat against Sunderland followed which left them in fourth place. Paradoxically, inconsistency came to be a given and, when the 2–1 home defeat by Everton on 19 January 1901 pushed Tom Watson's team down to eighth place in Division One, any hopes of making a mark in the Championship seemed to disappear. But it looked as if a fight for survival would be the raison d'être of Liverpool's season when the following week they were beaten by Bolton Wanderers.

First-round dismissal from the FA Cup by Notts County meant Liverpool had lost three successive matches. In mid-February, after eight defeats and 31 goals conceded, the Reds were in eighth place, nine points adrift of leaders Nottingham Forest, and the main task seemed to be to catch Everton who were three points ahead of them.

But, with five matches to play, on 13 April, deadly Lancastrian rivals Manchester City came to Anfield, and, despite a Billy Meredith goal, Liverpool won 3–1.

Nottingham Forest had headed the table for weeks but Liverpool gradually cut back their lead. After Sunderland won their last game of the season at Newcastle, everything depended upon

Liverpool's final game, played five days later against West Bromwich Albion at the Hawthorns.

In the final match of the season, a Monday-evening affair, on 29 April, the whole season balanced on Liverpool's potential to defeat the club that was pinned to the bottom of the League. Sunderland would benefit from any slip-up on Liverpool's part. Albion, who had only taken up residence at the Hawthorns the previous September (becoming the highest League club in England above sea level), had the hope to beat Liverpool and lift themselves from the foot of the table; the situation made the game a real battle.

The former Hearts player and Scottish international John Walker put Liverpool in the lead in the first half, following a Raybould shot that had been only half saved. For long periods during the game, the Throstles had laid siege to the Liverpool goal but the Anfield men had hung on. The Scousers won the Championship with a two-point gap between themselves and the Black Cats, although the Wearsiders had a much better goal average.

Liverpool hadn't lost a single game in their last dozen, dropping just three points, and only four goals went past Perkins. The away win at

Liverpool League Champions

	Pld	Home					Away					All games					Pts	GA
		W	D	L	F	A	W	D	L	F	A	W	D	L	F	A		
1 Liverpool	34	12	2	3	36	13	7	5	5	23	22	19	7	8	59	35	45	1.69
2 Sunderland	34	12	3	2	43	11	3	10	4	14	15	15	13	6	57	26	43	2.19
3 Notts County	34	13	2	2	39	18	5	2	10	15	28	18	4	12	54	46	40	1.17
4 Nottingham Forest	34	10	4	3	32	14	6	3	8	21	22	16	7	11	53	36	39	1.47
5 Bury	34	11	3	3	31	10	5	4	8	22	27	16	7	11	53	37	39	1.43
6 Newcastle United	34	10	5	2	27	13	4	5	8	15	24	14	10	10	42	37	38	1.14
7 Everton	34	10	4	3	37	17	6	1	10	18	25	16	5	13	55	42	37	1.31
8 The Wednesday	34	13	2	2	38	16	0	8	9	14	26	13	10	11	52	42	36	1.24
9 Blackburn Rovers	34	9	4	4	24	18	3	5	9	15	29	12	9	13	39	47	33	0.83
10 Bolton Wanderers	34	10	5	2	21	12	3	2	12	18	43	13	7	14	39	55	33	0.71
11 Manchester City	34	12	3	2	32	16	1	3	13	16	42	13	6	15	48	58	32	0.83
12 Derby County	34	10	4	3	43	18	2	3	12	12	24	12	7	15	55	42	31	1.31
13 Wolverhampton Wanderers	34	6	10	1	21	15	3	3	11	18	40	9	13	12	39	55	31	0.71
14 Sheffield United	34	8	4	5	22	23	4	3	10	13	29	12	7	15	35	52	31	0.67
15 Aston Villa	34	8	5	4	32	18	2	5	10	13	33	10	10	14	45	51	30	0.88
16 Stoke	34	8	3	6	23	15	3	2	12	23	42	11	5	18	46	57	27	0.81
17 Preston North End	34	6	4	7	29	30	3	3	11	20	45	9	7	18	49	75	25	0.65
18 West Bromwich Albion	34	4	4	9	21	27	3	4	10	14	35	7	8	19	35	62	22	0.56

Sunderland at the end of February had been the start of that crucial run.

Just eight seasons after joining the Football League, Liverpool were Champions, taking over the mantle from the great Aston Villa. The Reds had won 19 of their 34-game schedule, with seven matches drawn. They had scored 59 goals and let in 35, Sam Raybould being the club's leading marksman with 16 nets. As such, the Anfield side had gained more victories and scored more times than any other team in the Division. Indeed, throughout the League, only Grimsby, the Division Two Champions, had hit more goals (60). Just 18 players were used in Liverpool's title season, the impressive Raisbeck making all but three matches. He had been Liverpool's inspiration and the hero of the campaign, and after the Hawthorns win he was lifted on the shoulders of his teammates to hoist the Championship trophy.

For the *Liverpool Football Echo*, 'It did not look as if they had any prospects but when the old century closed the men bucked up.'

The side's return to Central Station, just before midnight that Monday, was greeted by thousands of supporters. A drum and fife band were playing 'The Conquering Hero' on the platform as the team's train pulled in. The new Champions carried the trophy through the crowded city streets. Once more Raisbeck was lifted shoulder-high, but this time the majority of his teammates received the same treatment, although big Tom Watson proved too much of a test even for the most jubilant supporters. There was an attempt to shoulder the club secretary, but it was said no one's arms were long enough to get round him and there was insufficient muscle power to get him off the ground.

Eventually making it back to Anfield during the very early hours of the morning, the Championship trophy was given pride of place in the old boardroom where, well into the small hours, it was appreciated by McKenna and William Houlding, John's son, who had succeeded him at Anfield.

Liverpool seemed set for a long period of glory and prosperity, attracting as they were the average attendance of 18,000. But after their amazing feats of 1901 Liverpool lost their way with the introduction of the £4 maximum wage (and a fixed signing-on fee of £10) on 1 April 1901. As they attracted relatively large crowds, Liverpool could well afford to offer their players good bonuses that could boost their earnings to £10 per week (this was said to be about the amount Liverpool players were earning each week in their Championship season). The new regulations effectively took away the advantages the club had earned by building a big supporter base. McKenna was always critical of the implementation of the maximum wage (which stayed in place until 1961). It led players to seek transfers and others to leave football completely and in 1904 the Reds were relegated. However, Liverpool retained Alex Raisbeck, paying him an 'extra wage' as the club's 'bill inspector'; part of his role was checking the advertisements around the ground.

The League promoted the new rules as an attempt to regulate the poaching of players that had been rife from before the League had been established, giving clubs equal opportunity to compete through the payment of a transfer fee. However, it was much more of a cost-capping exercise on the part of the clubs looking to minimise wages and maximise profits.

But it didn't take long for Liverpool to recover. They acclimatised to the new conditions and once again they came back up after one season and the club's second title win came in the 1905/06 campaign; Raisbeck and Raybould still remained from the club's last title-winning side. This made Liverpool the first club to win the Second and First Division titles in succession. In the process, the team hit 79 goals; Preston North End, four points behind the Reds, took the runners-up place. Joe Hewitt was Liverpool's leading marksman with 23 goals. The Anfielders won 27 of their 34 games with the outstanding Raisbeck again a key figure in the side, marshalling a sure defence (that let in just 25 goals) as Liverpool ran riot as an attacking force, scoring 93 times.

To complete a remarkable Merseyside double that season, Everton won the FA Cup after defeating Liverpool in the semi-final.

THE 1900/01 CHAMPIONSHIP SEASON MATCHES

The team line-ups are detailed as they appeared in the press reports researched (shirt numbers did not become obligatory until 1939). Some historians have recorded the teams according to modern formations: right-back at number 2 (second player detailed), outside left at number 11 (last player detailed). I have chosen not to do this as players often changed positions on the field at the time. (For instance, in Liverpool's first season in the Football League, Matt McQueen played in a number of positions including five matches in goal; he was to play between the sticks 37 times for the Reds in the club's first three seasons in the League. This made Matt the only man in English football history to have won Championship medals as both an outfield player and a goalkeeper.)

I hope by presenting the line-ups recorded in this way to provide the reader with some insight into the way the game was reported and perceived at the turn of the century.

1 SEPTEMBER 1900

LIVERPOOL (2) 3   **BLACKBURN R (0) 0**

T Robertson, Satterthwaite,
Raybould

The Liverpool side, except for the inclusion of John Robertson who took the place of Archie Goldie (who had moved to New Brighton Tower), was unchanged from the team that finished the previous campaign.

With 10 minutes played, Tom Robertson's excellent drive gave the home side the lead. Not long after this, a shot from John Cox went just wide. This was followed by a Charlie Satterthwaite header that Whittaker did well to save. A couple of opportunities fell to Oldham, but on both occasions Raisbeck blotted out the threat.

Just before the half-hour, Tom Robertson and Walker combined well with Satterthwaite, who finished the move to double his side's lead.

The second half was a more even contest. Somers went close to pulling one back for Blackburn and a dazzling rocket from the foot of Tom Robertson was put over the bar by Whittaker. With 80 minutes on the clock, Raybould's drive killed any hope Rovers might have had in reserve.

LIVERPOOL: Perkins; J Robertson, Dunlop, Wilson, Raisbeck, W Goldie, T Robertson, Walker, Raybould, Satterthwaite, Cox

BLACKBURN ROVERS: Whittaker; Crompton, Hardy, Hosie, Howarth, Houlker, Bryant, Somers, Oldham, Morgan, Kelly

ATTENDANCE: 20,000

REFEREE: Mr CC Fallowfield (Preston)

8 SEPTEMBER 1900

Stoke (1) 1

Maxwell

Liverpool (1) 2

T Robertson, Raybould

After winning the toss, Raisbeck chose to face the strong sun in the first half, taking the chance that it would probably be more of a problem late in the match. Stoke quickly grabbed the initiative and Benbow was only stopped by the crossbar. That seemed to be the signal for the hosts to commence a non-stop attack, which paid off after 20 minutes of play when Maxwell sent a crashing drive into a corner of the Liverpool rigging, although Bill Perkins nearly got to it.

For long periods, Stoke dominated, but a counter-attacking Tom Robertson broke through with a dramatic run that was finished off with a cannonball of a shot that only just went wide. This appeared to motivate the visitors and Walker's low drive that struck a post seemed to indicate that Liverpool felt they could get back into the match. This was proved to be the case just before half-time when Tom Robertson's shallow shot went between Wilkes's legs.

Liverpool then took command in the second half and on two occasions Cox came close to putting his side ahead. Satterthwaite was also unlucky. However, four minutes from time, the Anfield men claimed both points via Raybould.

LIVERPOOL: Perkins; J Robertson, Dunlop, Wilson, Raisbeck, W Goldie, T Robertson, Walker, Raybould, Satterthwaite, Cox

STOKE: Wilkes; Durber, Capewell, Bradley, Woods, Parsons, Johnson, Benbow, Higginson, Maxwell, Leach

ATTENDANCE: 10,000

REFEREE: Mr JC Tillotson (Birmingham)

15 SEPTEMBER 1900

Liverpool (2) 5   **West Bromwich Albion (0) 0**

W Goldie, Walker, Raybould (2),
T Robertson

Once more, the toss of the coin went the way of Raisbeck and he turned Albion into the sun. Undaunted, the visitors went for Liverpool from the first whistle and Roberts came near to opening the scoring. However, it was the host side that took the lead early on with a stroke of luck. Goldie tried a speculative long-range drive from the touchline and Reader, totally misjudging the Liverpool man's purpose, could only watch as the ball fell into the far corner of his net.

Charlie Wilson had a couple of chances prior to the moment when Raybould picked up a loose ball and sent it to Walker who went on a snaking dribble all the way through to his opponents' goal. Williams looked to have pulled one back for Albion from a free-kick but as the kick was indirect the score remained unchanged.

The visitors began to dominate and they showed all the signs of making Liverpool fight to hold on to their advantage. However, a clearance from Dunlop was gathered by Raybould and he lobbed it over Reader as the keeper moved to close him down. He darted round the floundering custodian to amazingly pick up his own pass and calmly slotted in his side's third of the game.

This seemed to destroy the Throstles' morale and Liverpool took control. Raybould once more ran on a loose ball and put it past Reader. In the last five minutes, it was Tommy Robertson who finished the game with a flourish.

LIVERPOOL: Perkins; J Robertson, Dunlop, Wilson, Raisbeck, W Goldie, T Robertson, Walker, Raybould, Satterthwaite, Cox

WEST BROMWICH ALBION: Reader; Adams, Williams, Dunn, Jones, Hadley, Chadburn, Pickering, Simmonds, Wheldon, Roberts

ATTENDANCE: 18,000

REFEREE: Mr GH Dale (Manchester)

22 SEPTEMBER 1900

Everton (1) 1   **Liverpool (0) 1**

McDonald   Raybould

A massive crowd witnessed a battle of a match contested at an incredible pace. Everton were awarded the first corner of the encounter and from this McDonald struck a peach of a volley to put the home side in front.

This seemed to steel Liverpool and they had the best of the play up to half-time. Almost instantly following the break, Cox won the ball and beat Wolstenholme, before crossing to Raybould. Watson could do little to prevent the visiting centre-forward from claiming the equaliser.

Apparently lifted, Liverpool went on a determined and sustained offensive and only Muir's excellent performance prevented at least three chances from being converted.

Players on both sides tired as the game went on. Perkins was forced to clear a mean drive from Sharp and in the last 10 minutes Everton sent in a barrage of shots looking for the winner, but the Liverpool keeper would not be beaten.

LIVERPOOL: Perkins; J Robertson, Dunlop, Wilson,

Raisbeck, W Goldie, T Robertson, Walker, Raybould, Satterthwaite, Cox

EVERTON: Muir; Balmer, Watson, Wolstenholme, Booth, Abbott, Sharp, McDonald, Proudfoot, Settle, Turner

ATTENDANCE: 44,324

REFEREE: Mr A Scragg (Crewe)

29 SEPTEMBER 1900

Liverpool (0) 1
Wilson

Sunderland (1) 2
Miller, Hogg

Neither side had been beaten in the League that season, so it was no surprise that a big crowd turned up to see this clash on a fine autumn day. The Liverpool team and formation remained unchanged (as it had since the start of the campaign). Sunderland fielded the same team that had fought out a draw with Aston Villa a week earlier.

The visitors slowly began to pressurise their opponents and Common and Miller both had opportunities prior to Miller gaining possession on the halfway line and dashing forward just a few strides to let loose a dynamic drive that found the corner of the home net.

Liverpool came out for the second half in a determined mood and kept Sunderland in their own half for long periods. The pressure paid off when Wilson lofted a great arching ball that dropped behind Doig and almost mystically curled into the top corner of the Wearsiders' rigging.

Not long after this, Wilson and Robertson, seemingly losing concentration simultaneously, gifted McLatchie with a shot; it was lucky that the effort struck a post. However, shortly before the end of the game, Hogg won it for the visitors and Liverpool dropped from second to fourth in the League table – Sunderland were in sixth place.

LIVERPOOL: Perkins; J Robertson, Dunlop, Wilson, Raisbeck, W Goldie, T Robertson, Walker, Raybould, Satterthwaite, Cox

SUNDERLAND: Doig; McCombie, Watson, Ferguson, McAllister, Farquhar, Hogg, Common, Miller, Livingstone, McLatchie

ATTENDANCE: 20,000

REFEREE: Mr JB Brodie (Stafford)

6 OCTOBER 1900

Derby County (2) 2

Goodall (pen), Boag

Liverpool (3) 3

T Robertson (2), Walker

County sent out their strongest side to face Liverpool; however, the visitors were obliged to bring in Andy McGuigan to fill in for Sam Raybould, who had sustained a big-toe injury. Derby were first on the offensive, Archie Goodall firing a fearful shot just 60 seconds after the kick-off. A determined drive from Raisbeck was the reply, although this sailed harmlessly over the crossbar.

Hugh McQueen, a former Liverpool man, brother of Matt, could only watch as his shot ricocheted off of Perkins's legs as the match swayed in favour of one side and then the other. But, when McQueen was fouled by Wilson, Goodall put the home side ahead from the resulting penalty.

Seemingly encouraged, Derby pressed forward, but a Cox dash along the wing concluded with a shot that Bromage couldn't control. Tom Robertson, swift to take advantage of the keeper's problems, forced the ball into the goal. Just minutes later, building on some fine play by the great Steve Bloomer, a volley from Boag restored Derby's lead.

However, Liverpool were able to respond in an instant, Tom Robertson once more pulling his side level in the 25th minute.

The visitors took control and a centre from Tom Robertson was met by Walker, who crashed the ball into the net. Shortly before half-time, Walker narrowly missed, heading just past a post.

Derby had the advantage of the wind behind them after the break and committed to a sustained attack for a lengthy period; May and Bloomer had fine opportunities, while Perkins flipped a Crawford drive over the bar. Liverpool had to deal with more than a few serious threats, including another Goodall penalty that hit the bar. In the dying minutes of the game, McGuigan had the ball in the net, but his effort was deemed to be offside.

LIVERPOOL: Perkins; J Robertson, Dunlop, Wilson, Raisbeck, W Goldie, T Robertson, Walker, McGuigan, Satterthwaite, Cox

DERBY COUNTY: Bromage; Methven, Blackett, May, Goodall, Leckie, Crawford, Bloomer, Boag, Wombwell, H McQueen

ATTENDANCE: 8,000

REFEREE: Mr GB Capes (Burton upon Trent)

13 OCTOBER 1900

Liverpool (1) 2   **Bolton Wanderers (1) 1**

Cox, Satterthwaite   Bell

The week before they arrived at Anfield, Bolton had achieved a fine victory over table-topping Aston Villa and a big crowd turned up to see what was expected to be a quality match. The Trotters, with just Sunderland beneath them and without a win before the Villa match, needed another positive result and were able to field their strongest side. However, their hosts had a worrying injury list including Raisbeck and Raybould so Maurice Parry made his League debut at right-half (he had joined the Reds from Brighton United in March 1900).

But it was a Parry miskick that led to Bell smashing a volley past Perkins with 15 minutes of the first half remaining. This was quickly followed by another blazing shot from Bell that Perkins managed to save.

On the cusp of the interval, Liverpool equalised. Woolfall messed up an attempt to clear his side's lines, seemingly provoking Sutcliffe to dash out to make amends, but Cox hit like a cobra to put the hosts level.

In the second half, Liverpool were dominant and Satterthwaite's fine drive, getting on the end of a cross from Walker, put the Reds in front. Rushing forward to defend his goal, Sutcliffe crashed into Satterthwaite and the Liverpool striker needed to be carried off the pitch, although his injuries were not as serious as they might have first looked.

That same afternoon at Gigg Lane, Bury got the better of West Bromwich Albion (6–1) and topped the League table. Liverpool were equal on 11 points with the new League leaders, although the Shakers had a better goal average.

LIVERPOOL: Perkins; J Robertson, Dunlop, Parry, Wilson, W Goldie, T Robertson, Walker, McGuigan, Satterthwaite, Cox

BOLTON WANDERERS: Sutcliffe; Woolfall, Halley, Fitchett, McAteer, Freebairn, Bell, Picken, McKie, Barlow, Tracey

ATTENDANCE: 12,000

REFEREE: Mr LW Furniss (Manchester)

20 OCTOBER 1900

Notts C (1) 3   **Liverpool (0) 0**

Ross, Morris, Bull

Liverpool started well enough and could have taken the lead from a shot by Cox that had to be headed clear. However, overall the start of the match told a tale of two sides evenly matched, each creating opportunities and providing an entertaining contest. Morris thought he had put County ahead but his effort was ruled offside. However, Ross threw himself through the visitors' defence to give the Magpies the lead with a 'gentle' shot.

Gee and Morris put in a fine performance for the hosts and Morris claimed a second goal with half-an-hour to play. Five minutes on, Bull put the game effectively out of Liverpool's reach and Notts County into third place in the League; Liverpool dropped from second to replace County in sixth.

LIVERPOOL: Perkins; J Robertson, Glover, Wilson, Raisbeck, W Goldie, T Robertson, Walker, Raybould, Satterthwaite, Cox

NOTTS COUNTY: Pennington; Lewis, Prescott, Ball, Bull, McDonald, Hadley, Warner, Ross, Morris, Gee

ATTENDANCE: 18,000

REFEREE: Mr WJP Whitsed (Grimsby)

27 OCTOBER 1900

Liverpool (1) 3
McGuigan, Cox, Raybould

Preston North End (2) 2
Dunn, Pearce

Preston came to Anfield struggling just above the relegation zone. Having won the toss, Raisbeck gave Liverpool the advantage of the near gale-force wind behind them. However, the home side were a goal down just 30 seconds into the match. Dunn's free-kick sailed into the goalmouth and Raisbeck helped the ball into his own net.

Quickly getting over what could have been a morale-sapping blow, Raybould and Robertson each carved out good chances prior to Cox making a fine a run down the left. Jim McBride failed to deal with the cross and McGuigan was quick to make the most of the North End keeper's mistake.

Raisbeck hit the Lilywhites' rigging soon after, but Walker had been in an offside position.

On the stroke of half-time, Pearce seized on a

mistake by John Robertson to shoot Preston into the lead for a second time.

With the change of ends, it was Liverpool's turn to deal with the hurricane conditions. However, they were in control of the game for the most part and squandered a number of opportunities before Tom Robertson's cross was met by the head of Cox to pull the Anfield side level.

In the dying seconds of the game, Raybould picked up the ball close to the halfway line and proceeded to dash through defenders as if they were ghosts. He finished a brilliant run with a spectacular goal. The result put Liverpool in fourth place – they were just two points behind League leaders Nottingham Forest.

LIVERPOOL: Perkins; J Robertson, Glover, Wilson, Raisbeck, W Goldie, T Robertson, Walker, Raybould, McGuigan, Cox

PRESTON NORTH END: McBride; Dunn, Holmes, Eccleston, McIntyre, Elliot, Smith, Pratt, Stevenson, Pearce, Henderson

ATTENDANCE: 12,000

REFEREE: Mr T Helme (Farnworth)

3 NOVEMBER 1900

Wolverhampton Wanderers (0) 2   Liverpool (0) 1

Bowen (2)   Walker

John Robertson appeared to be out of sorts and, with 10th-placed Wolves looking much the better team in the first half, it was only a great display by Perkins that kept the game goalless by the break.

Poppitt and Miller should have scored in the first part of the second period; however, against the run of play, a powerful close-range shot from Walker put the Reds in front.

Wolves replied after just 10 minutes; Bowen, meeting Miller's cross, struck though a melee of players. The home side applied the pressure after this but Liverpool seemed determined to hold firm and the game looked drawn. But, as the referee was reaching for his whistle, Bowen got his head to a last-gasp centre to deny the visitors a point. However, Liverpool hung on to fourth place in the League, although now four points adrift of Forest.

LIVERPOOL: Perkins; J Robertson, Dunlop, Wilson, Raisbeck, W Goldie, T Robertson, Walker, McGuigan, Raybould, Cox

WOLVERHAMPTON WANDERERS: Baddeley; H Davies,

Walker, Annis, Pheasant, Fleming, Poppitt, Beats, Bowen, Miller, Harcourt

ATTENDANCE: 12,000

REFEREE: Mr A Scragg (Crewe)

10 NOVEMBER 1900

Liverpool (3) 5

Raybould (2), McGuigan, Walker (2)

Aston Villa (0) 1

Johnson

Aston Villa came to Anfield on a cold but bright day in Liverpool as the team sitting in third place in the League, two points ahead of Liverpool. It was clear that the Reds needed to win this game if they were to prove to themselves and others that after a dozen games they were viable Championship contenders.

The home side took advantage of the powerful wind that was gusting down the park. Cox, having been selected to play for the Football League vs. the Irish League at Cliftonville, was replaced by Satterthwaite. Injury had ruled out Charlie Athersmith for Villa and the England winger was a big loss to the visitors.

Starting off on the offensive, Liverpool drew first

blood through a Raybould shot that George could have done nothing about. Raisbeck and John Robertson performed well in a Liverpool side that seemed to be working like a well-oiled machine and when McGuigan doubled the Reds' lead it felt like the inevitable had happened. A low hard drive from Walker sent the hosts in 3–0 ahead at half-time.

In the second half, Villa seemed to make some efforts to get back into the game but, when Raybould, having picked up a centre from the right wing, hit Liverpool's fourth, it looked all over for the visitors; their fate was confirmed when Walker struck again from a free-kick.

As the game rolled towards its end, Johnson gave his side some minimal solace, bettering Perkins from a corner. However, Liverpool had not closed the points gap between themselves and Nottingham Forest who now had lost just once in 12 League outings.

LIVERPOOL: Perkins; J Robertson, Dunlop, Wilson, Raisbeck, W Goldie, T Robertson, Walker, McGuigan, Raybould, Satterthwaite

ASTON VILLA: George; Noon, Spencer, Bowman, Pearson, Crabtree, Templeton, Devey, Garratty, Johnson, Smith

ATTENDANCE: 18,000

REFEREE: Mr F Bye (Sheffield)

17 NOVEMBER 1900

The Wednesday (3) 3   **Liverpool (2) 2**

Crawshaw, Wilson (2)   Raybould, Raisbeck

Liverpool arrived in Sheffield to face a side that had managed just nine points (only three wins) in 10 games and were just a couple of points outside the relegation zone.

The visitors ran at their Owlerton Park hosts from the off and this early pressure paid off when Cox sped along the wing to send a pinpoint pass to Raybould. The Reds' striker made no mistake after just three minutes' play. A shallow drive from the boot of Tom Crawshaw 10 minutes later made for a dramatic equaliser. Apparently inspired, the Owls attacked the Liverpool half in determined waves and it was Wilson's ferocious shot that gave Wednesday the advantage.

A spectacular run by Wilson followed by an immaculate shot sent Liverpool reeling. But Raisbeck rallied his troops and, regaining some composure, the Red horde went looking for blood; Raisbeck emerged from a fierce fracas to pull his side back into the game.

In the second half, both sides seemed totally committed to attrition at a manic pace. Wednesday had a spate of corners that produced a classic set of skirmishes around the Liverpool goal. As the 90-minute mark neared, Crawshaw, Wright and Cox, in an era long before substitutes were the norm, were among the walking wounded.

Liverpool slipped to fifth, still trailing Nottingham Forest by four points. They had 15 points, level with Aston Villa just below them (although the Birmingham side had played three more games than Liverpool).

LIVERPOOL: Perkins; J Robertson, Dunlop, Wilson, Raisbeck, W Goldie, T Robertson, Walker, Raybould, Satterthwaite, Cox

SHEFFIELD WEDNESDAY: Massey; Langley, Layton, Ruddlesdin, Crawshaw, Ferrier, Malloch, Wright, Wilson, Davis, McWhinnie

ATTENDANCE: 10,000

REFEREE: Mr T Helme (Farnworth)

24 NOVEMBER 1900

Newcastle United (1) 1   **Liverpool (1) 1**
Laidlaw   Cox

With the wind in his face, Raybould kicked off for Liverpool who seemed determined to take all the points from second-placed Newcastle. Looking to gain an early advantage from the whistle, Satterthwaite fired a shot in the first minute that was punched away by Kingsley. But, on the break, it was the Magpies who took the lead after just three minutes as Laidlaw fired in a superb drive.

Liverpool clawed their way back into the match and it was only the woodwork that stopped Raybould from equalising with a fine shot. However, with a quarter-of-an-hour of the first half played, Cox pounced on a loose ball and his ferocious shot left Kingsley helpless.

The visitors' commitment to attack at this point was unremitting. Only the head of Burgess prevented Satterthwaite from putting the Reds in front and Goldie, with a powerful blast, forced Kingsley to use his fists to clear his lines.

After the break, the home side claimed most of the ball, but without another goal the Tynesiders held on to their second place, while Liverpool stayed in fifth position sandwiched between and level on points with Manchester City (in sixth) and Bury (in fourth).

LIVERPOOL: Perkins; J Robertson, Dunlop, Wilson, Raisbeck, W Goldie, T Robertson, Walker, Raybould, Satterthwaite, Cox

NEWCASTLE UNITED: Kingsley; Burgess, D Gardner, Ghee, Aitken, Carr, Niblo, A Gardner, Peddie, MacFarlane, Laidlaw

ATTENDANCE: 17,000

REFEREE: Mr A Kingscott (Derby)

1 DECEMBER 1900

Liverpool (0) 1   **Sheffield United (1) 2**

Satterthwaite   Needham, Gilhooly

In the opening minutes, a shot from Cox went wide, but the Blades were quick to respond and it was obvious they had come ready to try to better their 13th position in the League and extend the three-point gap between themselves and the relegation places. Perkins did well to deny first Bennett and then Almond; Field also went close as the visitors charged forward.

But for a second it again looked like Liverpool would draw first blood when, with the keeper beaten, Satterthwaite's drive roared over Foulke's crossbar.

A centre by Bennett was gathered by Field; he jinked his way beyond John Robertson and cleverly passed back to Needham. The eloquently nick-named 'Nudger' let loose a terrific shot, worthy of his England international status, sending the ball flying into the corner of the home side's rigging.

With their passing leaving much to be desired, the high work rate of the Liverpool side was pretty much wasted and, even on the occasions when they did threaten to equalise, the gargantuan Willie 'Fatty' Foulke seemed impassable.

Starting the second half with some purpose, Red pressure obliged Foulke to punch away a deadly looking shot. The ball ended up with Satterthwaite who wasted no time in pulling his side level.

As the game reached its last seconds, Gilhooly claimed the winning goal. Liverpool, trailing League leaders Nottingham Forest by half-a-dozen points, moved uncomfortably into sixth position.

LIVERPOOL: Perkins; J Robertson, Dunlop, Wilson, Raisbeck, W Goldie, T Robertson, Walker, Raybould, Satterthwaite, Cox

SHEFFIELD UNITED: Foulke; Thickett, Boyle, Johnson, Morran, Needham, Bennett, Gilhooly, Almond, Field, Lipsham
ATTENDANCE: 15,000
REFEREE: Mr A Green (West Bromwich)

8 DECEMBER 1900

Manchester City (3) 3   **Liverpool (2) 4**
Smith, Cassidy (2)   Raybould, Cox, T Robertson,
                                   McGuigan

At City's Hyde Road ground, the home side kicked off three minutes before the programmed time, having the advantage of a light wind. The sides being level on points, the match promised to be a hard-fought affair.

With only nine minutes of the match played, a cross from the foot of Meredith was met by Smith, whose blazing drive entered the visitors' net well out of the reach of the flying Perkins. It took Liverpool something less than a minute to respond; Raybould's powerful shot leaving Williams stranded.

On the quarter-of-an-hour mark, cleverly bettering Dunlop's attempt to stop his progress,

Cassidy put his side 2–1 up. Both Dunlop and John Robertson looked something less than their usual competent selves as the Reds goal came under siege. But the visitors broke out down the right flank, Robertson carrying the game to City. This charge culminated in Cox placing Liverpool on level pegging with their hosts.

However, John Robertson was beaten by Dartnell and the resulting pass to Cassidy proved destructive; City's outside left restored the home side's lead.

The Manchester Blues, deploying the 'one-back game' strategy, constantly lured Liverpool into an offside trap and up to the break the Anfield men looked a frustrated crew.

Liverpool came out for the second half on the warpath and instantly Tommy Robertson equalised. Williams then was unable to hold a long-distance effort from McGuigan and for the first time in the game the Reds took the lead. Just minutes later, a Walker rocket was only denied by a post.

Liverpool remained in sixth place in the League, but now, just one place behind, Everton were threatening.

LIVERPOOL: Perkins; J Robertson, Dunlop, Wilson,

Raisbeck, W Goldie, T Robertson, Walker, Raybould, McGuigan, Cox

MANCHESTER CITY: Williams; Read, Jones, Moffatt, Smith, Holmes, Meredith, Ross, Gillespie, Dartnell, Cassidy

ATTENDANCE: 20,000

REFEREE: Mr T Helme (Farnworth)

15 DECEMBER 1900

Liverpool (0) 1   **Bury (0) 0**

Cox

With Bury's captain winning the toss, the visitors grabbed the benefit of the strong wind, a factor that put the damper on any ideas about basing the match on a precise passing strategy.

Early in the game Raybould looked threatening, but fourth-placed Bury had not come to Anfield planning to give much away and they certainly had the better of the first part of the match. Liverpool controlled the second half; Walker, Raybould and Tommy Robertson each had clear chances prior to Cox bettering Thompson as the keeper came forward trying to narrow the angle. Now just four points behind Forest, the Reds jumped into fourth place in the table, one point behind Aston Villa and one in front of Bury.

LIVERPOOL: Perkins; J Robertson, Dunlop, Wilson, Raisbeck, W Goldie, T Robertson, Walker, Raybould, McGuigan, Cox

BURY: Thompson; Leeming, McEwan, Wood, Pray, Ross, Richards, Reddish, McLuckie, Sagar, Plant

ATTENDANCE: 14,000

REFEREE: Mr F Kirkham (Preston)

22 DECEMBER 1900

Nottingham Forest (0) 0   **Liverpool (0) 0**

The visitors kicked off at 2.20 p.m. against the League leaders. This match threatened to be something of a dour confrontation, but in the end it was a tight game between two well-matched sides. A good opportunity was missed when Fred Forman lifted his shot high over the visitors' bar and both sets of players had chances to score, with Raisbeck showing fine form for Liverpool. As the encounter neared its conclusion, the home side came close to overwhelming the Reds but Perkins would not be beaten. Liverpool continued to trail

Forest by four points, but the Division One pacemakers were still three points clear of their nearest rivals Newcastle United.

LIVERPOOL: Perkins; J Robertson, Dunlop, Wilson, Raisbeck, W Goldie, T Robertson, McGuigan, Raybould, S Hunter, Cox

NOTTINGHAM FOREST: Linacre; Peers, Iremonger, Robinson, MacPherson, Frank Forman, Fred Forman, Capes, Calvey, Morris, Spouncer

ATTENDANCE: 6,000

REFEREE: Mr J Adams (Birmingham)

25 DECEMBER 1900

Liverpool (0) 0   **Derby C (0) 0**

The Rams won the toss and directed Raybould to kick off the match on what was a fine and uncommonly mild afternoon for a Christmas Day in Lancashire. The game was officiated by Bob Roberts, the ex-England international keeper.

Derby, given the side's personnel, seemed to be underachieving in 11th place in the League, but they imposed themselves on their visitors early on. However, it was Raisbeck (not for the first or last time) who came to the rescue of his side on a number of occasions. Hugh McQueen, a one-time Red, took the leading role in most of Derby's initial raids.

John Robertson made a goal-line clearance from a Boag shot in the second half as the game hurtled along at a tremendous rate. However, it seemed that both sides were trying too hard and much effort was expended with no concrete outcomes. But, with the other teams around them not playing, Liverpool jumped into second place in Division One.

LIVERPOOL: Perkins; J Robertson, Dunlop, Wilson, Raisbeck, W Goldie, T Robertson, McGuigan, Raybould, S Hunter, Cox

DERBY COUNTY: Fryer; Methven, Morris, Warren, Goodall, Leckie, Crawford, Bloomer, Boag, Wombwell, H McQueen

ATTENDANCE: 18,000

REFEREE: Mr R Roberts (Crewe)

29 DECEMBER 1900

Blackburn Rovers (3) 3   **Liverpool (1) 1**

Dewhurst (2), Whittaker   ·   Raybould

This match got off to an exhilarating start with Whittaker and Somers tearing along the right to send the ball to Dewhurst whose fantastic shot put the home side in front before the game finished its first minute. Although teetering precariously just above the bottom two on goal average in the League, Blackburn looked to be on fire and the form book seemed to be thrown out of the window when Fred Blackburn's centre was met by Arnie Whittaker to double Rovers' advantage.

The best work by the visitors came from Cox, but his effort went straight into the arms of Walter Whittaker. Not long after, Raisbeck was robbed and the way was left open for Dewhurst to make it 3–0 to the hosts. However, just before half-time Raybould gave the Reds some hope.

Liverpool probably shaded the rest of the match and Raybould had a couple of chances, but Rovers' morale had been boosted and there was no further score. Liverpool slid back into seventh place and now the gap between them and Forest had widened to five points, although the Anfield lads had a game in hand.

LIVERPOOL: Perkins; J Robertson, Dunlop, Howell, Raisbeck, W Goldie, T Robertson, McGuigan, Raybould, Satterthwaite, Cox

BLACKBURN ROVERS: W Whittaker; Haworth, Hardy,

Houlker, McClure, Moir, A Whittaker, Somers, Dewhurst, Morgan, Blackburn

ATTENDANCE: 8,000

REFEREE: Mr CC Fallowfield (Preston)

1 JANUARY 1901

Liverpool (1) 3	Stoke (1) 1
T Robertson, Cox, McGuigan	Whitehouse

Despite the glorious New Year's Day weather, the Anfield turf was still fairly heavy after recent rain. The Reds had departed Southport on the Monday morning before the Tuesday game. Plagued with injuries, struggling Stoke (in 15th place in the League, just a point above the relegation zone) were obliged to call half-a-dozen reserve players into their XI (four forwards and two half-backs).

The start of the game saw the visitors on the offensive but Liverpool took the lead on the quarter-of-an-hour after a cross by Cox was converted by Tommy Robertson's gracefully oblique shot; Liverpool's first goal of the 20th century.

However, errors by each of the Liverpool

full-backs allowed Whitehouse to equalise with a soft goal.

A penalty was awarded to the home side after Raybould had been stopped by Durbar. The decision looked a bit harsh and most of those present were surprised by the referee's verdict. However, Tom Robertson was unable to make the advantage stick, smacking the ball well past a post.

Following the restart, Wilkes was unable to hold a hard shot from Raisbeck and Cox was on hand to score. Now Liverpool were rampant in attack and McGuigan scored their third, picking up on Satterthwaite's cross.

LIVERPOOL: Perkins; J Robertson, Dunlop, Howell, Raisbeck, W Goldie, T Robertson, McGuigan, Raybould, Satterthwaite, Cox

STOKE: Wilkes; Capewell, Durbar, Parsons, Holford, Leech, Johnson, Whitehouse, Higginson, Harris, Lockett

ATTENDANCE: 15,000

REFEREE: Mr J Adams (Birmingham)

19 JANUARY 1901

Liverpool (1) 1　　　　　　**Everton (1) 2**

Cox　　　　　　　　　　　Taylor (2)

On a soaking-wet afternoon, the toss was won by Settle and the Reds were set to defend the Oakfield Road goal. With 20 minutes played, Taylor's vicious shot was too much for Perkins. However, this was followed by a promising combination of Tom Robertson and McGuigan, but this died as the ball came to a halt in a huge puddle, allowing Crelley to clear Everton's lines.

The visitors were adapting quicker to the demanding conditions but, with eight minutes of the first half to play, following a shot from Taylor that went just wide, Robertson's cross got past both Eccles and Booth for Cox to dart in and equalise. It seemed that the home side smelled blood and Tommy Robertson found the back of the net. However, Walker was deemed to have handled and Robertson's effort was to no account.

For the second half, both sides donned clean shirts and captains Settle and Raisbeck talked about the possibility of abandoning the match as the conditions were starting to look dangerous.

However, a Sharp centre connected with Taylor to put Everton in front and, as such, from that moment on there was not much of a chance that the visitors would want to walk away from a winning position.

Following an indirect free-kick, Eccles looked to have put the Toffees further ahead, but the ball hadn't touched a second player so no goal was awarded.

With 23 minutes left to play, the three officials debated the merits of continuing with the game, but the Anfield crowd's demands of 'Play the game!' seemed to sway the decision and the match was played out. Both sides had chances but in the end Liverpool dropped to eighth position as Everton drew a point and a place clear of their neighbours.

LIVERPOOL: Perkins; J Robertson, Dunlop, Wilson, Raisbeck, W Goldie, T Robertson, McGuigan, Raybould, Walker, Cox

EVERTON: Muir; Eccles, Crelley, Wolstenholme, Booth, Abbott, Sharp, Taylor, Proudfoot, Settle, Turner

ATTENDANCE: 18,000

REFEREE: Mr A Scragg (Crewe)

16 FEBRUARY 1901

Bolton Wanderers (1) 1   **Liverpool (0) 0**

Bell

Liverpool faced deeply troubled Lancashire rivals Bolton who had just Preston beneath them, having lost 12 of their 22 games (although they had been defeated just once at home). On a pitch that was in awful condition, Goldie on two occasions passed up scoring opportunities before Wanderers started to find their feet and Picken threw away a golden chance to open the scoring. With both sides threatening, Liverpool were the first to hit the net. Unfortunately, it was direct from an indirect free-kick and as such no goal was given. The visitors continued to pressurise their hosts, but Sutcliffe seemed equal to every challenge, frustrating Raybould, Satterthwaite and McGuigan in turn.

Bolton turned the tide but McKie, looking all but through, was brought to ground; however, the ball strayed to the feet of Bell whose drive ricocheted off a post before crossing the line with 10 minutes of the first half to play. As the initial period came to its conclusion, an upright denied Raybould and, as Mr Barker put the whistle to his lips, Bell's apparent goal was deemed offside.

Liverpool fought hard to get back on level terms in the second half, but Sutcliffe could do no wrong, despite the best efforts of Cox and Raybould. Perkins prevented McKie from extending the Trotters' lead but Bolton were in control, as Picken's shot went fractionally too high.

The season seemed to be drifting away from Liverpool. Nine points behind Nottingham Forest, the priority seemed to be to try to catch Everton, three points and two places above them in sixth.

LIVERPOOL: Perkins; J Robertson, Dunlop, Wilson, Raisbeck, W Goldie, T Robertson, McGuigan, Raybould, Satterthwaite, Cox

BOLTON WANDERERS: Sutcliffe; Somerville, Brown, Freebairn, McAteer, Fitchett, Tracey, Barlow, McKie, Picken, Bell

ATTENDANCE: 10,000

REFEREE: Mr AJ Barker (Hanley)

23 FEBRUARY 1901

Sunderland (0) 0   **Liverpool (0) 1**

Cox

The Reds faced a Sunderland side that were holding second place in the First Division just two points behind leaders Nottingham Forest. But undaunted the visitors came at their hosts with offensive intent. However, yet another in-form keeper stood in their path – Ted Doig played a blinder. But, as the game reached its last stages, Doig was forced to punch a shot away and Cox hit what was to be the only goal of the encounter, the keeper having totally committed himself. Raybould nearly grabbed a last-gasp goal but hit a post.

Liverpool clambered to seventh place but were still seven points adrift of Forest.

LIVERPOOL: Perkins; Glover, Dunlop, Wilson, Raisbeck, W Goldie, T Robertson, Walker, Raybould, Satterthwaite, Cox

SUNDERLAND: Doig; McCombie, Watson, Ferguson, McAllister, Jackson, Hogg, Farquhar, Gemmell, Livingstone, McLatchie

ATTENDANCE: 11,249

REFEREE: Mr JH Strawson (Lincoln)

2 MARCH 1901

Preston North End (1) 2   **Liverpool (1) 2**

Becton (2)   Satterthwaite, Raybould

A strong wind and a stinging drizzle that interfered with the vision transformed Deepdale into a swamp. The conditions, together with Preston's rock-bottom status, resulted in a less than modest crowd.

Bill Dunlop hit the back of the net, but not for the first time that season the effort had come from an indirect free-kick and, as the ball had not been touched by another player after the man who initially struck it following the original foul, no goal was given.

Satterthwaite concluded a fine run with a low hard drive to put Liverpool in the lead after 20 minutes. Preston seemed to wilt and the Anfield men had a hatful of chances before ex-Liverpool man and England international Frank Becton pulled the Lilywhites level in the dying seconds before the break.

At the start of the second half, Preston came out determined and on a sustained offensive. Thankfully for the Reds, Perkins held off the rampant

North End attack with a fine display of the keeper's art. With less than half-an-hour left on the clock, Liverpool once more took the lead courtesy of Raybould but Becton was quick to reply via a Pratt cross and the game ended with honours even.

Everton did their neighbours an unintentional favour defeating Nottingham Forest 4–1 at Goodison. But Sunderland got more of the advantage, taking over at the top on goal average; Liverpool remained in seventh place, seven points behind the leading pair.

LIVERPOOL: Perkins; Glover, Dunlop, Wilson, Raisbeck, W Goldie, T Robertson, Walker, Raybould, Satterthwaite, Cox

PRESTON NORTH END: McBride; McMahon, Dunlop, Todd, McIntyre, Elliott, Green, Becton, Gara, Pratt, Rodgers

ATTENDANCE: 1,500

REFEREE: Mr T Helme (Farnworth)

ANFIELD RISING

9 MARCH 1901

Liverpool (0) 1   **Wolves (0) 0**

Raybould

Liverpool were back at Anfield in the League for the first time for seven weeks facing a side with just a three-point cushion between themselves and relegation. Billy Beats kicked off as Wolves played towards the Oakfield Road goal.

The first half was shaded by the home side but the Reds didn't manage to convert this into goals. After the break, Liverpool had to start a man short as Satterthwaite had picked up a knee injury late in the first half. Wolves made the most of the situation but were held off by the ever reliable Raisbeck.

Satterthwaite, having returned to the fray after treatment, had a shot cleared by Baddeley but when the ball fell to Raybould the Anfield striker made it count, although Liverpool's lead was not confirmed until the referee had finished a lengthy debate with a linesman.

Forest's 0–0 draw with Sunderland allowed Liverpool into sixth place, 0.06 on goal average behind Everton.

LIVERPOOL: Perkins; Glover, Dunlop, Wilson, Raisbeck, W Goldie, T Robertson, Walker, Raybould, Davies, Satterthwaite
WOLVERHAMPTON WANDERERS: Baddeley; Walker, Barker, Fleming, Pheasant, Annas, Miller, Wooldridge, Beats, Harper, Bowen
ATTENDANCE: 14,900
REFEREE: Mr Ditchfield (Burslem)

16 MARCH 1901

Aston Villa (0) 0   Liverpool (1) 2
                           McGuigan, S Hunter

Aston Villa were a point behind Liverpool and therefore had every incentive to win this match, but they were still involved in the FA Cup, which threatened to be something of a distraction for the Villans. It was a grey and chilly day in Birmingham, and, perhaps with the Cup in mind, the home side sent out half-a-dozen reserve players to face a Liverpool team also lacking some influential first-teamers, including Raybould (who would score for the Football League in the 6–2 win over the Scottish League at Ibrox that same day) and Satterthwaite (who was still carrying the injury picked up in the game with Wolves the week before).

Half-an-hour in, Walker's cross was collected by McGuigan and his effort sloped just under the crossbar.

Villa hit back but Perkins was again Liverpool's wall. 'Sailor' Hunter gave his side a 2–0 win in the last second of the game.

Sunderland's 2–0 defeat of Blackburn Rovers took them a point clear at the top of the League. Liverpool, although equal on points with Everton and Bury above them, remained in sixth place on goal average. Hopes of Championship glory now looked, at best, remote, as with just eight games left the Reds were still five points behind the increasingly confident Black Cats.

LIVERPOOL: Perkins; Glover, Dunlop, Wilson, Raisbeck, W Goldie, T Robertson, Walker, McGuigan, S Hunter, Cox

ASTON VILLA: Whitley; Noon, Aston, Bowman, Cowan, Pearson, Lloyd, Devey, Garratty, Bache, Templeton

ATTENDANCE: 14,000

REFEREE: Mr A Kingscott (Derby)

23 MARCH 1901

Liverpool (1) 1 **The Wednesday (0) 1**
Raybould Spiksley

In 11th place in the First Division but six points clear of relegation, Wednesday had little to play for but, that said, the Reds performed as well as they had all season following Stubbs's save from a fine header by Cox. Continued assaults produced a dangerous shot from Raybould that went fractionally wide of the target.

But Wednesday got themselves back into the match, Miller going close to giving the Owls first blood.

Tom Robertson, presented with an open goal, missed badly and Stubbs did well to save a determined drive from the boot of Hunter. However, the rebound was picked up by Raybould and it looked like a fatal stroke of luck until the visiting keeper somehow managed to scoop the ball away.

Five minutes from the half-time whistle, Raybould's shot was deflected by Layton to put the home side ahead.

After the break, the match reverted to

something of a midfield battle and from one of many free-kicks (this particular one had been given against Wilson) the ball glided into the goalmouth. A mix-up between Perkins and Glover resulted in a feeble clearance by the keeper. England international Fred Spiksley took advantage and pulled the sides level.

The Owls came forward in determined onslaughts, but once more Raisbeck was a Red rock. Hunter put Cox through a number of times, but Gosling kept the left-winger tightly manacled. Miller saw an outstanding chance saved magnificently by Perkins, while a shot from Cox went a yard wide in the very last seconds.

LIVERPOOL: Perkins; Glover, Dunlop, Wilson, Raisbeck, W Goldie, T Robertson, Walker, Raybould, S Hunter, Cox

THE WEDNESDAY: Stubbs; Layton, Gosling, Ferrier, Crawshaw, Ruddlesdin, Davis, Chapman, Miller, Wright, Spiksley

ATTENDANCE: 12,000

REFEREE: Mr GF Allwood (Wolverhampton)

30 MARCH 1901

Liverpool (1) 3   **Newcastle United (0) 0**

S Hunter (2), Walker

Because Raisbeck had been selected to play for the second of his eight Scottish international appearances (that day the oldest international game finished in a 2–2 draw at Crystal Palace) and Wilson was out injured, Liverpool were obliged to revamp their half-back line. Newcastle's centre-half Aitken had also been called up for Scotland (the first of his 14 caps).

The game was just minutes old when Gardner's shot went narrowly wide. Tom Robertson responded for the Reds with a drive that Kingsley could only clear for a corner. Raybould's drive was well on target, but was blocked and Walker and Robertson both saw chances whiz past the uprights.

The Magpies' pressure resulted in a couple of corners in quick succession. However, John Glover was performing well and the threat was snuffed out. Cox went close twice before Raybould and Burgess contested a long ball and, as the rain poured in torrents, it was Hunter who dashed in to put Liverpool in front after 25 minutes.

ANFIELD RISING

The home side doubled their lead after Cox opened the Newcastle defence for Walker to score. However, the Tynesiders seemed to regroup and made several seriously threatening attacks. But as the game matured the visitors looked tired and appeared to be focusing on keeping the score down rather than developing ambitions to get back into the match.

Liverpool pressure continued but it wasn't until a few minutes from the end that a fine cross from Robertson found the head of Hunter who gave the Reds their third.

Liverpool were still five points adrift of Sunderland at the top of the table, but they were three points behind Forest who now seemed in striking distance and Liverpool fans could justifiably hope for the runners-up spot at the end of the term.

LIVERPOOL: Perkins; Dunlop, Glover, Parry, T Hunter, W Goldie, T Robertson, Walker, Raybould, S Hunter, Cox

NEWCASTLE UNITED: Kingsley; D Gardner, Burgess, Carr, Innerd, Ghee, Eraser, Heywood, Peddie, MacFarlane, A Gardner

ATTENDANCE: 10,000

REFEREE: Mr F Kirkham (Preston)

8 APRIL 1901

Liverpool (0) 1   **Notts County (0) 0**
Raybould

Although most people would have said that both sides were out of the Championship race, which seemed to be very much a two-horse affair between Sunderland and Nottingham Forest, the two teams meeting in a gale at the Liverpool ground that day could feasibly claim second or third place and as such a lot of status and some pride.

After Cox's shot was saved, Raisbeck sent a rocket of a drive over the bar. The wind was ruining any chance of developing a passing game and was blowing shoots way off target, but Dunlop's accurate free-kick went straight into the arms of Pennington. Cox generated a fine move but his concluding drive missed narrowly.

This episode was followed by a sustained attack by the Magpies. However, Perkins was on fine form; one save from a corner was brilliantly executed, while Raisbeck and Dunlop fought like lions to hold off the rampaging visitors.

Liverpool responded and, after Raybould's header went just wide, Walker saw his fine shot go past a post. More chances came via Dunlop and Walker but Liverpool could not translate the pressure into goals, even though County, having lost Morris, had to play the last quarter-of-an-hour of the first half with 10 men.

After the interval, the visitors were back to full strength with Morris returning to combat and they committed everything to attack. Perkins saved a blistering shot from Ross before Cox, Walker and Robertson hit back. But Ross's drive so nearly broke the ice; the effort was just fractionally too high with Perkins beaten.

But, with the last quarter-of-an-hour approaching, the hosts were awarded a throw-in close to the corner flag. Raybould hit the ball on the volley and his thunderbolt justly won the game.

LIVERPOOL: Perkins; Glover, Dunlop, Parry, Raisbeck, W Goldie, T Robertson, Walker, Raybould, S Hunter, Cox

NOTTS COUNTY: Pennington; Lewis, Montgomery, Ball, Bull, McDonald, Hadley, Warner, Ross, Morris, Gee

ATTENDANCE: 15,000

REFEREE: Mr A Green (West Bromwich)

13 APRIL 1901

Liverpool (3) 3

T Robertson (2), Cox

Manchester City (0) 1

Meredith

The injury-hit Manchester Blues came to Anfield very much a rearranged troop. Gillespie kicked off, Manchester City attacking the Oakfield Road goal. A Holmes foul resulted in a free-kick and Walker came close to getting the better of Williams. It was another free-kick that led to the opening goal. Tom Robertson comfortably beat Williams following a move that linked Cox, Raybould and Walker. Within a minute, the Reds were 2–0 up – Cox getting the goal for Liverpool.

Hunter released Raybould who found the net but the centre-forward was ruled offside. Raybould was not cowed and moments later shot wide.

City came back into the match, mostly thanks to the skill of Billy Meredith. He looked certain to score but a last-ditch Dunlop tackle stopped any further progress.

Just before the break, Tom Robertson hit the Reds' third.

Eight minutes from the whistle, Meredith scored a consolation goal for City after he went by

Dunlop with consummate ease and Liverpool's claims for offside went unheeded by Mr Horrocks.

LIVERPOOL: Perkins; Glover, Dunlop, Parry, Raisbeck, W Goldie, T Robertson, Walker, Raybould, S Hunter, Cox

MANCHESTER CITY: Williams; Jones, Read, Holmes, Smith, Moffatt, Dougal, Cassidy, Gillespie, Scotson, Meredith

ATTENDANCE: 14,000

REFEREE: Mr R Horrocks (Farnworth)

20 APRIL 1901

Bury (0) 0   **Liverpool (0) 0**

The Shakers' home record, losing just three of their 17 matches at Gigg Lane, scoring 31 goals and conceding 19, demonstrated the task Liverpool had in travelling to their Lancashire rivals on a hot day for football.

After winning the toss, Bury chose to play with the light wind in their favour.

A drive from McLuckie looked dangerous but went wide and this seemed to motivate the visitors, Raybould and Raisbeck both having chances.

Bury won the first corner of the match; however, Goldie comfortably cleared any threat, hoofing the ball up to Cox. Something looked on for the Reds' flying winger but he was stopped in his tracks by Darroch, who was having a fine game.

Following good opportunities for Robertson and Walker, Wood saw two creditable efforts go wide.

In the second half, Bury seemed to be in control and favourites to take the day but Liverpool managed to earn a point in what had proved to be a hard-fought confrontation.

With two games in hand, Liverpool were just two points behind Sunderland but still in fourth place with both the Nottingham clubs heading them. But what had looked an impossible dream just a couple of weeks previously now felt like a definite possibility. Other teams' results had gone Liverpool's way while they appeared to have put together a run of form just at the right time, having not lost since mid-February.

LIVERPOOL: Perkins; Glover, Dunlop, Parry, Raisbeck, W Goldie, T Robertson, Walker, Raybould, S Hunter, Cox

BURY: Montgomery; Darroch, McEwan, Pray, Leeming, Ross, Richards, Wood, McLuckie, Berry, Plant

ANFIELD RISING

ATTENDANCE: 8,000

REFEREE: Mr F Kirkham (Preston)

22 APRIL 1901

Sheffield United (0) 0   **Liverpool (2) 2**

Raybould, Satterthwaite

While the Blades were only four points clear of the relegation places, they had a couple of games in hand over the two teams immediately below them. However, no one could deny that they needed points. Their visitors just had to win to maintain their title-winning ambitions, as anything less would be leaving too much to chance. But the following Saturday the side they were confronting at Bramall Lane were scheduled to meet Tottenham Hotspur in the FA Cup Final replay, so their collective mind would certainly have been on that event (although Spurs would ultimately prevail 3–1).

Walker's solid shot was punched clear by Foulke before Tom Robertson tore along the right to cross. Raybould didn't hesitate and sent the ball crashing into the rigging. Little more than a moment later, Satterthwaite's powerful volley proved to be the blow that brought the home side's morale crashing down.

Liverpool were well in command for the rest of the half, their hosts feeling the lack of England defender Ernie Needham.

After the break, United were limited to just a couple of attempts on the Reds' goal.

Liverpool left Sheffield in second place in the League with the same points as Sunderland but with a game in hand over the Wearsiders. However, with both Nottingham clubs still in the race, the final two games of the season were going to be crucial, particularly Liverpool's next one against Nottingham Forest.

LIVERPOOL: Perkins; Dunlop, J Robertson, Parry, T Hunter, W Goldie, T Robertson, Walker, Raybould, Satterthwaite, Cox

SHEFFIELD UNITED: Foulke; Thickett, Boyle, Johnson, Morran, Wilkins, Beers, Barnes, Almond, Priest, Lipsham

ATTENDANCE: 6,000

REFEREE: Mr JC Tillotson (Birmingham)

27 APRIL 1901

Liverpool (1) 2   **Nottingham F (0) 0**

Cox, W Goldie

The opening minutes saw both teams come close to going ahead and it was hard to separate the teams prior to the home side pressure forcing several corners. With MacPherson off the field injured, skilful work from Satterthwaite and Cox laid the ground for a Robertson shot that crashed against an upright. The ball rebounded to Cox who made no mistake putting his side in front.

Satterthwaite, Robertson, Walker and Raybould all had chances before half-time. Forest continued with 10 men as Calvey restarted the match. But Dean and Capes pressed forward. However, a goalmouth scramble concluded with Goldie hitting the Reds' second. This was quickly followed by Raybould netting, having picked up on a fine pass from Cox; but 'Sam the man' was ruled offside.

Liverpool were performing exhibition stuff and it was only Linacre's fine form that kept the score as it was; the Forest keeper was applauded by even the most biased Reds fans.

Liverpool's destiny was now entirely their own

responsibility. They were in second place, level on points with Sunderland. No one could catch them now as all six of the other top-seven clubs had played all their fixtures. A draw or a victory in their last game against rock-bottom West Bromwich Albion two days later would win them the League Championship.

LIVERPOOL: Perkins; J Robertson, Dunlop, Parry, Raisbeck, A Goldie, T Robertson, Walker, Raybould, Satterthwaite, Cox

NOTTINGHAM FOREST: Linacre; Iremonger, McCurdy, Timmins, MacPherson, Robinson, T Forman, Murray, Calvey, Capes, Dean

ATTENDANCE: 20,000

REFEREE: Mr T Armitt (Leek)

29 APRIL 1901

Liverpool (1) 1   **West Bromwich Albion (0) 0**

Walker

The Reds were understandably eager to attack and soon after the start Reader was forced to save from both Walker and Raybould before Goldie's shot went just the wrong side of an upright.

Liverpool dominated the initial period and inevitably took the lead when Raybould gathered a pass from the left and hit a belter that Reader could only partly block. The Baggies' keeper stumbled as John Walker ran on to the loose ball to score an historic goal.

Almost instantly Walker again found the back of the net but he was called offside.

The home side threw themselves into a committed assault and Pickering's drive had to be headed away for a corner by John Robertson.

Albion came at Perkins from every angle but the Liverpool defence was steadfast, although Garfield came close, firing over the bar.

The Throstles seemed to be getting the better of things and it looked as if the Reds might be denied the League title at the last hurdle in the most unlikely of circumstances (at home to the bottom club). Stevenson's effort was well judged by Perkins (his positioning made sure it went straight into his arms) and Pickering charged the keeper, sending the Reds' custodian crashing to the dirt as he cleared the ball.

It seemed the West Brom forwards were intent on dragging Liverpool down with them. However,

Dunlop and Robertson were equal to them and allowed Liverpool to set up a break on the left, but it culminated in Walker's shot being comfortably saved by Reader.

This seemed to spark something of a Liverpool revival and Robertson was caught offside just when the Albion goal looked at his mercy.

West Brom worked hard to respond but their visitors fought to maintain their advantage to become Football League Champions for the first time, just eight years after joining the League. Albion were condemned to relegation with Preston. The scenes of jubilation and excitement as the Reds left the pitch would be remembered for lifetimes.

LIVERPOOL: Perkins; J Robertson, Dunlop, Parry, Raisbeck, W Goldie, T Robertson, Walker, Raybould, Satterthwaite, Cox

WEST BROMWICH ALBION: Reader; Adams, Chadburn, Perry, Jones, Hadley, Roberts, Pickering, Stevenson, Wheldon, Garfield

ATTENDANCE: 4,000

REFEREE: Mr Baynton (Wolverhampton)

CONCLUSION

John McKenna was connected with the League administration for 34 years. He was elected to the League Management Committee in 1902 and became its vice-president in 1908, and he was Football League president from 1910 until he died at the age of 82 on 22 March 1936. He was also a vice-president of the Football Association.

It was once written that McKenna 'fought straight, never shirked an issue, and ever sort to be just. His concern for the poorer clubs was constant and sincere. With him, power was only a weapon to administer government wisely and judicially.'

His bold signing of a troop of 13 Scottish players to bolster Liverpool for their first season of

League football was typical of the man's bravado and enterprise. He brought the likes of George Allan, the first Liverpool player to be capped by Scotland, and Frank Becton, an England forward, to the club. He was responsible for Alex Raisbeck becoming a Red, a player who would be forever ranked among Liverpool and Scotland's greatest ever players.

Tom Watson had a 19-year managerial career at Anfield up to 1915, an era that saw some of the greatest players in Liverpool's history take to the Anfield pitch. He oversaw the first League Championship win and the club's first FA Cup Final appearance. Raisbeck, Goddard, Parry, Wilson, Doig, Robinson and Fleming, as well as trainer Billy Connell, were the pallbearers at Watson's funeral on 11 May 1915.

During renovation work on the Sandon Hotel in 1986, a mosaic of Alex 'Sandy' Young kitted out in the Everton colours of salmon-pink shirt and navy-blue shorts was discovered; this homage is believed to have been commissioned as recognition of Young's goal that won the club its first FA Cup 80 years earlier. The mosaic was donated to Everton by the owners of the Sandon

Hotel and stands proudly in one of the function rooms at Park End, Goodison Park. But the Sandon had been John Houlding's 'castle'. He had been a founding father of both Everton and Liverpool.

As the pages above show, the split that created these two sides of what was essentially the same coin has a slightly different genesis than what is generally portrayed. Houlding is usually presented as a sort of Rachman figure, holding a beleaguered Everton to ransom at a rate that threatened to destroy the club. But this is hardly believable. Why would a shrewd businessman like Houlding want to kill the goose that laid the golden egg? If he had pushed Everton to financial extinction at Anfield, he would have ended up with a redundant, albeit state-of-the-art football ground, the very asset that motivated him to create Liverpool FC.

When one looks objectively at the facts and the wider context of football at the end of the 19th century, the discerning researcher is left with only one realistic explanation for Everton's abandonment of Anfield. While it is undoubtedly true that Houlding's motivation for involvement in football was substantially (although certainly not wholly) based on the intention of making a profit, it seems clear that the faction who walked away from Anfield also wanted to make money – their efforts to strip Anfield of its fixtures and fittings is just the most obvious evidence of this. Mahon was an accountant and businessman and he, like the rest of his crew, may have been as interested in revenue as Houlding seemed to be. The problem may have been that they didn't just want a slice of the cake; they may have wanted their own cake. This, of course, would have been fair enough, but this possibility has hardly been acknowledged. Perhaps by leaving Anfield with the name and most of the personnel of what had become a proven power in English football at a time when the game was booming, Mahon and his allies may have taken the most advantageous action for themselves at an optimum time. They certainly quickly confirmed their usurpation and monopoly of the top-class football business in the city by establishing a limited liability company in that name. What happened in 1892 was a corporate coup that it seems was meant to leave Houlding and his camp at Anfield with nothing but a huge liability. Out of that, Houlding, McKenna and Barclay were expected to undertake at best a salvage operation from which Mahon and his supporters may have hoped to draw further advantages. As it was, the spirit and soul they were unable to carry off across Stanley Park evoked a latent twin clad in the blood-red livery of Liverpool Football Club.

The development of red and blue aspects of Liverpool football reflected the start of a new mass leisure industry, which we would clearly recognise today. Although relatively impoverished by today's standards, over the latter part of the 19th and the first part of the 20th century, in Liverpool and across the UK, there were improvements in housing and, as a consequence, health. This brought with it a growing labour force which had slowly become more educated. Alongside the increased mechanisation of industry, this allowed for higher wages (and thus a better diet for workers) and increased time off work.

Most significantly, people + cash + time, in a society of the type that bloomed in the late 19th century, presented a situation that had to be taken advantage of; it was an opportunity to be exploited. The self-made Houlding had seen this coming very early on and it appeared Mahon and his allies, mostly from staunchly middle-class backgrounds, were not prepared to watch a mere publican take the lion's share. The final deal 'King John' proposed to Everton would not only have made him a fortune, but it would also have ensured a monopoly for the club in Liverpool, not something that men, bred of the ethic of competition, would have seen as particularly profitable for them personally (relative to Houlding and possibly the Orrells when the shares were finally divided out). They appear to have wanted their own pot.

All this is not saying that Houlding and Mahon and McKenna etc. did not care about football, they clearly did, but they were simply not men to separate their enthusiasm from their driving passion that had made them extraordinary enough people to be able to create great entities like Liverpool and Everton Football Clubs. Like Gus Mears at Chelsea or Henry Norris at Arsenal, these individuals did very little in their lives that wasn't primarily about making money; they would have seen this as part of their achievement – it was not as exceptional to create a successful football team as it was to develop an accomplished club that at the same time sat above its peers as a financial triumph. Indeed, as transfers, professionalism and ground development began to dominate football, success became entwined to mean both financial and on-field excellence.

John Houlding passed away in the South of France during 1902 at the age of 70. He had been an energetic servant of the club for nearly two decades, although during his last years his activity had been limited. When his funeral cortege made its way through the streets around Anfield and Everton, sombre locals stood bareheaded, and the flags at both Goodison and Anfield were lowered to half-mast in respect and as a tribute to 'King John' and his association with both teams; players from Everton and Liverpool were his pallbearers. He may not have died a hero of Evertonian folklore but it cannot be denied he has to be remembered as one of the great creators of Merseyside football.

Time, it is said, heals all wounds. Football is a uniting force in the last analysis and we are capable of being bigger than our past. It is to be hoped that, rather than exaggerating differences based on historic feuds, football supporters in the city of Liverpool can replicate the kind of solidarity it showed in response to the murder of Rhys Jones in 2007 – I for one was moved to tears when for the first time Everton's 'Z-Cars' was played at Anfield. Differences eventually fade and in the last analysis our common links in the gift of loyalty and need for identity make us all one – the only positive that can be drawn from being torn apart is to come back together.

In the end, football is about hope and Liverpool's rise from the ashes was one of the greatest expressions of what hope can do in football. But as a new season starts it all begins again, tomorrow, next week, next Saturday, look to Liverpool and over the Mersey you might detect a deep-red glow as once again the world will see *Anfield Rising.*

EPILOGUE

Liverpool Football Club means: The world to me, I see it like a second family. I somehow feel so connected to everyone who shares my love of the Reds. It all began about 25 years ago when I was about five years old. I grew up in a house of Liverpool fans so it only seemed natural to cheer on the likes of Souness, Rush and King Kenny Dalglish.

Growing up in the eighties was an amazing time as a Reds fan; one of my earliest memories came on 6 November 1982 at Goodison when Ian Rush (who has the same birthday as me) scored a hat-trick in a 5-0 win over our fiercest rivals Everton.

My favourite ever player in a Liverpool shirt was John Barnes; he was like a masterful wizard with the ball at his feet and I dreamed of being just like him.

The history of the club is second to none, with a wealth of world-class players and a more than impressive trophy cabinet. Knowing where it all started, how and why it happened is important for those with a strong connection with the club; like understanding who you are and where you are from; identity is wrought in the first times of all things.

When I was asked to write this piece on what Liverpool Football Club meant to me, only one word came to mind ... PROUD!

Wayne Virgo, lifelong Red

LIVERPOOL TIMELINE

1878 The St Domingo's Football Club is founded.

NOVEMBER 1879 At a meeting at the Queens Head Hotel in Village Street, off Everton Road, it is decided to rename the club Everton Football Club.

20 DECEMBER 1879 The team play their debut match at Stanley Park vs. St Peter's; the 6–0 result is Everton's first win.

1880 Everton become members of the Lancashire Association.

1882 Priory Road becomes Everton's home pitch.

John Houlding starts to become a significant figure in the club.

OCTOBER 1883 The first official match is played at Priory Road.

MARCH 1884 The club win their first trophy, the Liverpool Cup.

John Houlding is appointed club president.

27 SEPTEMBER 1884 Everton play their debut game at Anfield against Earlestown and win 5–0.

1885 Everton become a professional club.

1886 Everton's first involvement with the FA Cup. Everton are drawn to meet Glasgow Rangers but withdraw.

15 OCTOBER 1887 Everton make their first 'real' foray into the FA Cup. They are beaten 1–0 in the first round by Bolton Wanderers but after an appeal the game is replayed and the Trotters are eventually defeated 2–1 at Anfield.

ANFIELD RISING

1888 Everton become founder members of the Football League.

FEBRUARY 1888 The FA stage a Cup semi-final at Anfield, the first time the city of Liverpool has been given such an honour. The match between Crewe Alexandra and Preston North End attracts a crowd of about 10,000; Preston win 5–0.

24 JULY 1888 The club's executive committee ask for a lease on Anfield.

AUGUST 1888 William E Barclay becomes Everton's club secretary.

8 SEPTEMBER 1888 Everton make their League debut in front of 10,000 supporters at Anfield, vs. Accrington. The home side win 2–1.

1889 Anfield stages its first international (England vs. Ireland – England win 6–1).

22 MAY 1889 Club members make an official resolution at a special committee meeting that the club should become a limited liability company with the aim of purchasing Anfield. This resolution is not adopted.

SEPTEMBER 1889 Richard Molyneux takes charge of team matters at Anfield.

APRIL 1890 Liverpool dock workers win the half-day Saturday.

1891 Everton win the League Championship.

15 SEPTEMBER 1891 John Houlding lays out his plan for the formation of a limited liability company at a general meeting at the Royal Street Hall.

25 JANUARY 1892 At the College, Shaw Street, during a special general meeting, it is confirmed that Houlding's plans for a limited liability company will not be accepted.

Under the leadership of George Mahon (a committee member), Everton move to Goodison and become a limited liability company.

FEBRUARY 1892 At an Everton committee meeting, the resignations of Houlding and Barclay are accepted.

ANFIELD RISING

15 MARCH 1892 Houlding, the Everton president, is effectively dismissed.

MAY 1892 John Houlding re-registers his club as the 'Liverpool Association Football Club and Athletic Grounds Company Limited'. Houlding is elected president of the new club, while Barclay becomes club secretary working alongside club director John McKenna.

The Football League rejects Liverpool's request for membership.

3 JUNE 1892 A special resolution and the seal of approval by the Board of Trade takes effect and Liverpool Football Club are officially born.

1 SEPTEMBER 1892 Liverpool Football Club play their first match, a friendly vs. Rotherham Town at Anfield. Liverpool win 5–1.

15 OCTOBER 1892 In the FA Cup first qualifying round, Liverpool defeat Nantwich at Jackson Avenue 4–0.

15 APRIL 1892 Liverpool win the Lancashire League.

22 APRIL 1893 The very first Merseyside derby takes place – the final of the Liverpool Cup – Liverpool win 1–0.

1893 Liverpool are elected to Division Two of the Football League.

2 SEPTEMBER 1893 Liverpool Football Club play their debut match game in the Football League at the Paradise Ground against Middlesbrough Ironopolis and win 2–0.

9 SEPTEMBER 1893 Anfield stages its first Football League game vs. Lincoln; Liverpool win 4–0.

APRIL 1894 Liverpool win the Second Division Championship and promotion to the First Division.

13 OCTOBER 1894 The first Liverpool League derby takes place at Goodison – Liverpool lose 3–0.

17 NOVEMBER 1894 Anfield stages its first Liverpool derby in the League, a 2–2 draw.

APRIL 1895 Liverpool are relegated to the Second Division.

APRIL 1896 Liverpool win the Second Division Championship and are promoted to the First Division.

AUGUST 1896 Tom Watson, the secretary of Sunderland (the 'Team of all the Talents'), is recruited as Liverpool's club secretary-manager.

1897 At the age 65, John Houlding stands down as club president and is replaced by his son William.

MARCH 1897 Liverpool reach the semi-finals of the FA Cup for the first time and are defeated 3–0 by Aston Villa.

20 FEBRUARY 1897 Henry (Harry) Bradshaw becomes Liverpool's first full international player when he is selected to play for England against Ireland.

MARCH 1899 Liverpool reach semi-finals of the FA Cup.

APRIL 1899 Liverpool finish as runners-up in the First Division.

APRIL 1901 Liverpool win the League Championship.

1902 John Houlding dies aged 70.

BIBLIOGRAPHY

I have made reference to a number of texts to illuminate statistics, facts, individual player details and match reports. I have also called on national newspapers, club and supporters' handbooks, soccer annuals, programmes featuring the club, various football magazines, club histories and Who's Who publications relating to other clubs. Autobiographies and biographies of other players and managers have informed the work as have football reference books used to confirm details.

As in most historic research, one comes across contradictory information. In some cases, I have been obliged to make judgements about what is most probable, given the contextual information.

Alcock, C.W. & Hill, R. (eds) (1997 reprint) *Famous Association Footballers 1895/96* Yore

Barwick, B. & Sinstard, G. (1988) *The Great Derbies: Everton v. Liverpool* BBC Books

Belton, B. (2003) *Founded on Iron* Tempus

Belton, B. (2006) *War Hammers* Tempus

Belton, B. (2007) *Scottish International Football Miscellany* Pennant Books

Belton, B. (2008) *Birth of the Blues* Pennant Books

Belton, B. (2008) *Red Dawn* Pennant Books

Belton, B. (2008) *The First Gunners* Pennant Books

Bickerton, B. (1998) *Club Colours* Hamlyn

Buckland, G. (2007) *Everton Strange But Blue* Sport Media

Butler, B. (1987) *The Football League 1888–1988. The Official Illustrated History* Queen Anne Press

Clareborough, D. (2001) *Sheffield United Football Club – 100 Greats* The History Press

Cook, C. & Stevenson, J. (1988) *Modern British History* Longman

Corbett, J. (2003) *Everton: The School of Science* Pan

Davies, G.M. & Garland, I. (1991) *Welsh International Soccer Players* Bridge Books

Fabian, A.H. & Green, G. (eds.) (1961) *Associated Football* Caxton

Farror, M. & Lamming, D. (1972) *A Century of English International Football 1872–1972* Robert Hale

France, D., King, P. & Sheehan, D. (1999) *Gwladys Street's Hall of Fame* Skript

Gibbs, N. (1988) *The Football Facts* Facet Books

Gibson, A. & Pickford, W. (1905) *Association Football and the Men Who Have Made It* (4 vols) Caxton

Goldsworthy, M. (1969) *The Encyclopaedia of Association Football* Robert Hale

Goldsworthy, M. (1972) *We Are The Champions* Pelham Books

Graham, M. (1986) *Everton* Hamlyn

Green, G. (1953) *The History of the Football Association* The Naldrett Press

Harding, J. (1991) *For the Good of the Game: The Official History of the Professional Footballers' Association* Robson

Hargreaves, I. (1989) *Liverpool Greats* John Donald

Hill, J. (1978) *Great Soccer Stars* Hamlyn

Hodgson, D. (1979) *The Everton Story* Arthur Barker

Horsnell, B. & Lamming, D. (1995) *Forgotten Caps* Yore Publications

Hutchenson, J. (1982) *The Football Industry* R. Drew

Inglis, S. (1985) *Soccer In The Dock* Willow

Inglis, S. (1988) *League Football and the Men who Made It* HarperCollinsWillow

Inglis, S. (1996) *Football Grounds of Britain* HarperCollinsWillow

Johnston, F. (ed.) (1934) *The Football Encyclopedia* Associated Sporting Press

Joyce, N. (2004) *Football League Players' Records 1888 to 1939* SoccerData

Keates, T. (1928) *History of the Everton Football Club, 1878–1928* Thomas Brakell

Keith, J. & Thomas, P. (1975) *The Daily Express A–Z of Mersey Soccer* Beaverbook Newspapers Ltd

Kelly, S.F. (1987) *Forever Everton* Queen Anne Press

Kelly, S.F. (1993) *The Anfield Encyclopedia* Mainstream

Kelly, S.F. (1997) *You'll Never Walk Alone –
The Hamlyn Illustrated History of Liverpool,
1892–1997* Hamlyn/Reed International
Books Ltd

Knighton, L. (1950) *Behind the Scenes in Big
Football* Stanley Paul

Lamming, D. (1987) *Who's Who of Scottish
Internationalists: 1872–1982* AFS

Mallory, J. (1997) *Football League Tables* Collins

Mason, T. (1980) *Association Football and
English Society 1863–1915* Harvester Press

Matthew, T. (2006) *Who's Who of Liverpool*
Mainstream

Mearns, A. (1883) *The Bitter Cry of Outcast
London: An Inquiry into the Condition of the
Abject Poor* Leicester University Press

Needham, E. (2003 reprint of 1901 original)
Association Football Soccer Books

Oliver, G. (1995) *World Soccer* (2nd ed) Guinness

Onslow, T. (2002) *Everton FC: The Men From the
Hill Country* Countyvise

Pead, B. (1988) *Liverpool: A Complete Record
1892–1988* Breedon

Pead, B. (1990) *Liverpool: Champions of
Champions* Breedon

Phillips, D. (2003) *Liverpool Football Club: An A–Z* Aureus

Phythian, G. (2005) *The True Story of William Foulke* Tempus

Pickard, A. & W. (1905–06) *Association Football and the Men Who Made It* (4 vols) Caxton

Platt, M. (2003) *The Essential History of Everton* Headline

Ponting, I. (1996) *Liverpool: Hamlyn Player By Player* Hamlyn/Reed Consumer Books

Ponting, I. (1998) *Everton Player by Player* Hamlyn

Pringler, A. & Fissler, M. (1996) *Where Are They Now?* Two Heads Publishing

Prole, D. (1964) *Football in London* Robert Hale

Shaoul, M. & Williamson, T. (2004) *Forever England – A History of the National Side* Tempus

Roberts, J. (1978) *Everton: The Official Centenary History* Granada

Roberts, K. (1998) *Goodison Glory* Breedon

Rogers, K. (1989) *Everton Greats* Sportsprint Publishing

Rogers, K. (1998) *100 Years of Goodison Glory* Breedon Books.

Ross, I. & Smailes, G. (1985) *Everton: A Complete History* Breedon Books

Smith, B. (2007) *The Blue Correspondence* Countyvise

Spiller, R. (ed.) (1990) *AFS Football Who's Who: 1902–03, 1903–04, 1907–08, 1909–10* AFS

Taylor, R., Ward, A. & Williams, J. (1993) *Three Sides of the Mersey, An Oral History of Everton, Liverpool and Tranmere Rovers* Robson Books

Wall, F. (1935) *Fifty Years of Football* Cassel & Co.

Wall, F.J., Alcock, C.W. et al. (1906) *The Book of Football* Amalgamated Press

Walvin, J. (1975) *The People's Game. A Social History of British Football* A. Lane

Wigglesworth, N. (1996) *The Evolution of English Sport* Frank Cass

Young, P. (1963) *Football On Merseyside* Stanley Paul

JOURNALS/NEWSPAPERS
Athletic News
Charles Buchan Football Monthly
Daily Express
Daily Journal
Daily Mail
Daily Mirror
Daily News and Leader
Evening Post
Football Chat
Football News
Football Players' Magazine
Football Sun
Liverpool Daily Post
Liverpool Echo
Liverpool FC handbooks, reviews, magazines,
supporters guides
Liverpool FC official programmes
Liverpool Review
Liverpool Tribune
The Field
The Footballer
The Times
The Sportsman
The Weekly Herald

Saturday Night and Football Sun
Soccer History
Sporting Chronicle
Sunday Pictorial
Sports Times

OTHER PUBLICATIONS

Topical Times annuals
Association of Football Statisticians (AFS)
Bulletin (various)

ARCHIVES ETC.

1837online.com
British Library
British Library Newspapers
British Pathe
Liverpool Libraries
Guildhall Library
University of Leicester
National Football Museum, Preston